OUTLAW BIKER

OUTLAW BIKER

My Life at Full Throttle

RICHARD "DEADEYE" HAYES
with Mary Gardner

CITADEL PRESS
Kensington Publishing Corp.
www.kensingtonbooks.com

CITADEL PRESS BOOKS are published by

Kensington Publishing Corp.
850 Third Avenue
New York, NY 10022

All Kensington titles, imprints, and distributed lines are available at special quantity discounts for bulk purchases for sales promotions, premiums, fund-raising, educational. or institutional use. Special book excerpts or customized printings can also be created to fit specific needs. For details, write or phone the office of the Kensington special sales manager: Kensington Publishing Corp., 850 Third Avenue, New York, NY 10022, attn: Special Sales Department; phone 1-800-221-2647.

First printing: March 2008

10 9 8 7 6 5 4
Printed in the United States of America

Library of Congress Control Number: 2007937046

ISBN-13: 978-0-8065-2899-1
ISBN-10: 0-8065-2899-0

I would like to dedicate this book to my very dear friend and co-author Mary Gardner—who entered my world (the world of Harleys, violence, sex, drugs, and rock 'n' roll), saw past the facade, and got to know the real people—for believing I could write the book and for putting up with my terrible spelling and penmanship. I lived it, but she helped me bring it to life.

Thanks,
Deadeye

Acknowledgments

Thanks to Edie, Jessica and Danielle, my brother Bill Hayes, and all my club brothers. Also a special thanks to Cripple Mike at Butch's Custom Cycle and to Fred from Yarusso Bros. for that great eggplant parmigian.

—Deadeye

Thanks to Bill Dorn and Bill Hammond of the 2Bills Agency, to Michaela Hamilton for riding editorial shotgun, to Gary Niemeier, who provided computer skills for the manuscript, and to Sue Kearns and Jim Kuether for their photography skills.

—Mary

Foreword

Here is what you need to know first about *Outlaw Biker: My Life at Full Throttle.* It's a true story. So get ready for an adventure with a one-of-a-kind writer, a fifty-six-year-old, one-eyed, multi-tattooed Buddhist Harley biker, member of the Los Valientes Motorcycle Club in Saint Paul, Minnesota. He's standing behind me right now, wondering how I learned to type so fast.

Deadeye wrote his manuscript in pencil or ball-point on legal pads, backs of shopping lists, old notebook paper. At first he tried to type it on a computer, but the printer was broken. Writing the old way was easier, and that's how the rest of the book got done.

I'm a seventy-year-old woman who, about six years ago, dropped in on Butch's Custom, a Harley Davidson repair and customizing shop in Saint Paul, to see if I could hang out in the back room. I wanted to learn enough about Harley mechanics to make the bikers in a novel I was writing sound like they knew what they were doing. Butch let me in, and in the course of the three years I spent dropping in to see him, Mother Mick, and Gaylord, I learned a tiny bit about Harley engines and a lot about bikers. While I was there, I made myself popular with the contribution of homemade cookies. I also picked up a few tantalizing tidbits about Deadeye, who was Butch's best friend, club brother, and apparently the best storyteller in the biker community.

I never met Deadeye, though, until after Butch died, and Deadeye was working to help close down the shop for Sandy, Butch's widow. She introduced us. Then, later, when I had to find someone to write a blurb for the dust jacket of *Salvation Run,* my biker novel, I thought of Deadeye. I called him, and he came up to my condo to take home the manuscript. "I was afraid I wouldn't like it," he said later, but he did, even though the copy of the manuscript I'd given him was missing three pages, and they contained the scene where the biker and his lady finally connect in bed. "I *thought* maybe something wasn't there," Deadeye said after I figured out what had happened and restored the missing pages. The blurb, once I corrected Deadeye's dyslexic spelling, was wonderful.

Salvation Run was published by the University Press of Mississippi in 2005, and Deadeye was game to help me with publicity, bringing the Harley he'd built in memory of Butch to the Midwest Booksellers Association convention in Saint Paul and doing readings with me at various bookstores. Several other Los Valientes members sat in the audiences just to hear Deadeye perform. We'd practiced together at my condo, and he'd put in some extra time at home. We turned out to be quite a team.

Then I was asked to be present at the Loft, the literary center in Minneapolis, to participate in a discussion of how to publicize your own book. Deadeye and I mostly sat on the sidelines ("Get a biker" didn't seem like very practical advice to me), but afterward he drew lots of attention from the female audience. One of the ladies came up, ran her finger down his arm to his spiderweb tattoo, and said, "What's that?" Deadeye replied, "My website." I knew then that he could become a writer.

Later that evening, when we were sitting in the lobby outside the classroom, I said, "Deadeye, you know what? We work together well. I think we should put together your autobiography. You could write down chunks from your past just as they came to you. Then you could read what you wrote back to me, and I'd ask you for any details that seemed to be missing. After that, I'd take your manuscript, type it up, fix the spelling and paragraphing and all that stuff. It might be fun."

"People keep saying I should write the story of my life," Deadeye said, tattoos gleaming. "It must be karma. Let's do it."

And we did. Here it is.

—Mary Gardner

OUTLAW BIKER

The rain pounded against the windows at that little truck stop off I-90 as I looked around at my midnight dining companions. Two truckers at the counter were in a deep conversation about which truck stop had the best lot lizards. Then there was the retired couple on their way to visit grandkids in New Mexico. (I picked that up from their conversation with the waitress, who seemed genuinely interested.) Finally there was the six-top of party animals. Somehow I felt completely at home in this nomad environment.

I guess I could have avoided the rain and bad weather by riding down in the van with the rest of the guys, but it wouldn't have seemed right to show up at Slim Jim's funeral in a cage. Just four days ago he was enjoying the Arizona sun and highways when lights out. He probably didn't even see the chick on the cell phone roar through the stop sign, turning that cherry '42 Knucklehead into scrap metal and my brother into road kill.

Jim and I didn't come down the same chute or have the same dad or even wear the same patch, but we were brothers in every sense of the word. Two beat up 'n' beat down scooter tramps, old school to the bone.

Well, coffee done, waitress tipped, leathered up. One kick and that Evo Rigid roared "More road!" as I popped her into gear, pointed toward Flagstaff, and throttled up. Even in the downpour and lightning, it just seemed right—no easy ride down or easy good-bye.

My mind drifted back to the last run Slim Jim and me made together several years ago. . . .

CHAPTER 1

ON THE ROAD

Damn, there goes the alarm. Man, I hate working Saturdays, but that's the fun of owning your own business. I'd better at least stop by the clubhouse to see everyone off—that's the least the club president can do.

I hate missing runs. All the shit I get from the guys, and then I really feel left out afterward when they're all talking about the fun they had. But at least they have a great day. It smells so good after last night's rain. It's got to be 75 already, and it's only 8 a.m.

As I ease the chopper onto Highway 52, I start looking around and notice how blue the sky is today—the white of the clouds almost looks fake. Woooh, better pay attention to the road! That van just cut over with no signal. Dickhead. I'd give him the finger, but why start the day with negative karma?

Coming up to Marian, I see two bikes ahead and throttle up. Sure as shit, it's Burp and Jim on their way to the clubhouse. As I catch up, they wave and smile. As we turn onto Western, I can feel the excitement. Everyone is really psyched. Last night everyone was showing up, dropping off tents, sleeping bags, everything they didn't want to strap to their bikes. After all, we had the Big Blue Bus as a backup vehicle, and we could get a lot of shit in it—three kegs and ice with at least two cases of booze and steaks, as well as four bikes. There was even room for a couple of us to sleep if there was a storm. We were set.

We came around the corner and backed up to the curb. Mother Mick yelled, "You better have a talk with that prospect! He showed up with bagels instead of rolls. What the hell—even some cream cheese shit! We had to send him up for rolls. Needledick New Yorker!"

I slid off the bike and wandered into the clubhouse where I was met by Gaylord, the road captain, saying, "Are we going to leave on time at ten a.m. or dick around until eleven or twelve?"

I said, "No, get everyone gassed up and leave at ten. Anyone not here knows the route and has to play catch-up."

I grabbed a roll and walked over to Butch and Tooter. They started with, "Oh, the president has to work and can't hang around with us, has to make that big money."

"Yeah," I said, "it sucks being responsible. When you have a restaurant and you are open certain hours, you have to be there." Then I went upstairs to see if Beaver was there, and we sat down and went over the route. As vice president, he was in charge when I wasn't there. I got Gaylord, and we went over the details. I told him to brief everyone before we left as to the route and make sure to tell the invited guests to ride behind the prospects. He said there was road construction on the route last week, but he had a shortcut already mapped out. During all this, I think I heard fifteen times that they wished I was going along. It was hard to see all the commotion and not want to be a part of it.

At 9:40 we were all outside, and Gaylord was giving the specifics. There were about forty people with the invited guests, and I was bummed, knowing I would be at work and they would be out cruising. I was going to catch up after work, but there was nothing like leaving with the pack. The sound, the roar, was deafening—man, you got goose bumps. It made the ground shake—nothing like it.

Well, everyone was gassed up and the bus was loaded. It was a good investment for $2,000. The bikes were lining up, and I'd gone around shaking hands and saying, "Have a great ride. I'll be there tonight."

But I'd only gotten halfway through the line when I walked over to my own bike, kicked it over, and before I knew it, I was at the head of the line. Beaver laughed and said, "I knew you couldn't just watch us leave, Bro."

"What's a few less burgers and tacos?—it isn't like it's brain surgery," I said. "I'll call in at the first gas stop and tell them the kitchen is closed today because of sickness." (I was sick of working.)

Then Sizzler pulled up to stop the traffic on Western, and off we went. I looked in my mirrors just to watch the bikes keep coming around the corner. The rush you feel is too cool, up in front, leader of the pack, watching the looks on the faces of the people in their General Motors cages as we roll by. This is living.

As we roll onto 94, we throttle up, and the sound is great. We head into the middle lane, tighten up into a nice pack, and off we go. You feel so alive on a bike with the wind pounding your body and every crack in the road coming up to meet you. All your senses are heightened. I like to play back the events of the previous days, or maybe play a little Bob Seger in my head like "Turn the Page" or "Roll Me Away." When I look back in my mirror, I see all these bikes and know I'm a part of this. We are all together, all brothers.

How many people look at us rolling down the road and say, "Man, I wish that was me." But they know deep down that, though it looks great, it's not for them because there's too much to lose.

At our first gas stop, we fill all the pumps, but I get everyone over to the one island, leaving the second one open for the citizens. After all, I don't want people to get the wrong impression. Then Dirty Don comes up bitching how much oil Red's bike is throwing at him, and he's covered with it. So I say, "Tell it to the road captain. He's in charge while we're on the road." Soon everyone gets done gassing up and grabs a snack, and thirty minutes later we're off on our way north. We were heading up to a campground a little past Annandale where we'd spend the night. The trip goes smooth, and when we get to the town, we decide to stop and see what's going on. You'd think we all had three heads and were on drugs, the way people stared. But the town looked kind of cool with a Western motif on the front of all the little shops.

We all piled into the first bar, when someone said, "Let's go eat." I think the bartender mentioned a smorgasbord up the street, so I sent a prospect to see who wanted to eat and round them up. The rest of us would be in the bar waiting. I was one of the eaters, along with fifteen others, and I also had the money because the club was paying and the treasurer was out of town. I left $150 in the bar for the non-eaters, so everyone was happy.

The eaters did well at the smorgasbord. When it was time to pay, everyone was going through the line, and they all told the cashier that "Crime" was paying and pointed to the back where I was. Finally, when I got up to the till, she asked me if I was "Crime," and I thought I'd have some fun, and said, “Yes,” to see what this was all about. She handed me a bill for $190.15, and I just stood there for about a minute, then looked her right in the eyes and said real serious-like, “Didn’t anyone ever tell you crime doesn’t pay?” The look on her face took all the humor out of it because she really thought I meant it. I was afraid she was going to cry, so I pulled out the money and gave it to her, even with a $10 tip for her troubles.

I think some of the patrons must have thought we had never eaten before, the way everyone chowed. I mean, we have several members who could be competitive eaters—Evo, Burp, and Mother Mick can do some serious damage. Sometimes I really get a kick out of people. Their first impression of us is “O shit, hide the women and small animals,” but then they are quite surprised that we are almost human. We use utensils and all, and everyone is polite and courteous unless provoked.

However, if provoked, we can put on quite a show. I remember three years ago when me, Mother Mick, Dirty Don, and Hambone were at a Red Lobster. It took them fifteen minutes to seat us even though almost no one else was in the place. Finally we got seated next to two couples as plastic as Barbie’s and Ken’s parents. The way they were acting with side glances and snickers, you’d think we’d beat Grandma and raped the poodle. They even called the seater and asked if they would move us, but no luck, here we were to stay.

So I asked Mick, loudly, if he’d cleaned up that pesky crab problem, and he just laughed and said that he was housebreaking them. That got a good laugh from our table, but not theirs. Then as the food came, I started to talk about how I got my Red Wings the first time. Hambone, the prospect,

asked what Red Wings are—he really didn't know. I told him it was when you performed oral sex while the woman was on the rag. I thought he was going to lose it, and the yuppies were just staring straight ahead—I think they were in shock. I don't think they blinked for five minutes during our conversation about the different types of Wings (Red, Brown, Yellow).

Then I got up to use the loo, and on my way back, I stopped at their table, said "Hi," and pulled up a chair like we were old friends. I told them we were on our way to a party and they were more than welcome to join us. I noticed they weren't really eating (I guess their eyes were bigger than their stomachs), and there was a lobster tail that wasn't touched. I said, "Are you going to eat that?" and Dave (as I found out his name was) said, "No, here, have it," so I grabbed it and ripped it out of the shell and ate it with my bare hands as we talked. After what I bet seemed like hours to Dave, Pat, Jim, and Victoria (those were their yuppie names), they said they had to be leaving and asked the waitress to bring the check. When it came, I grabbed it, paid, and tipped the waitress, which I think shook them up more than anything else I'd done. They just thanked me and said they would have to pass on the party, what with babysitters and all. And that was the end of their Big Bad Biker Encounter.

But back to the run to Annandale. At the bar, things had gotten a little out of hand. Fast Jack was racing up and down Main Street with his Wolfman mask on. Butch had cleaned out the pull tab boxes. They couldn't believe how he hit all the winners in three boxes, but that's Butch. Several of the guys had become too friendly with the waitresses, and their boyfriends had taken offense, but not the girls. Then someone said, "The cops are here." I walked out and was met by this very large sheriff asking who was the head honcho. I said I could help him. I was informed that they wanted us to leave town posthaste, and I said, "Sure, we're on our way to so-and-so campground."

"I want you to leave the county, not just the town," he said.

Just then Fast Jack did a wheelie past the bar, still wearing his mask. The sheriff just looked at me and said, "Several more sheriffs and highway patrol cars will be here shortly to escort you out." I told him that we'd be ready in twenty minutes. So I got everyone together to tell them our new plans (which I didn't even know), when Sizzler said his dad had a place not far from here. I figured that was great even if it's in this county, because it's private land. So we saddled up, and with two sheriff cars ahead of us and two behind, plus highway patrol backup, we started out. They had the streets blocked, so we shot straight out of town. They followed us for about three miles, then turned off.

So we went on to Sizzler's dad's place, which was only about twelve miles away. His dad was real glad to see his son and all his playmates, and we set up camp across the road from his house. In about half an hour, the fire was going, the bar was set up, food was cooking, and the music was blaring. I was just sitting back in my lawn chair with a big Windsor coke, looking around and thinking, Man, can it get any better than this? A beautiful day for a run, everyone together, no accidents or arrests, and now a great place to party. Yeah!

After everyone ate and the fire was stoked, someone said something about a barrel race, and before we knew it, a course was set up. Well, a barrel race would have been a good idea several drinks earlier, but we still had about ten

bikes in it. We all took turns racing down about a quarter of a block, turning around the keg, and racing back to the start. Tooter was using Michael's bike, and he ran down and ran into the keg, which set the tone nicely. Gaylord, the road captain, went down and spun out and got the longest time. This went on for about an hour until it got dark.

Then we all entered serious party mode. For some reason, the whole campground was overrun by frogs. I was telling people that when I retired, I was going to breed frogs for fishing, and that they were really good for guard frogs. This got a strong reaction. The guys couldn't usually tell when I was serious or bullshitting, but I said, "No, they have frog ranches where you herd them, and you have little lassoes and branding irons. You can train them to attack." Mother Mick said, "Man, you are all sooo full of shit."

"No, really, this is true," I said.

Well, there was this frog on the table right in front of Mick by the lantern. Mick bends down and gets right in the frog's face and says, "Oh, look, what a ferocious frog!" But just then the frog jumps right in his face. Mick stumbles back with the frog stuck to his face—he's shitface drunk—and falls on his back, his arms and legs flailing, screaming his head off. We all lost it—me and Burp fell to the ground laughing. I mean it took five minutes for us to compose ourselves. I even pissed myself. Just the sight of Mick with the frog in his face!

When we all settled down, Burp asked Mick if he'd seen the fangs on that frog. "I think he was going for your jugular," he said.

All Mick would say was, "Real funny, assholes."

After that, when I was walking to our bus, I saw Dirty Don by Tooter's car. (He had brought Doc up in his '66 Chevy ragtop—Doc couldn't ride a bike anymore, but he was a brother.) The passenger door was open, and Don had one hand on the roof. As I got closer, I could see he was so trashed he was pissing into the car. I yelled "Holy shit!"

He just stumbled back and said, "What?"

I think it was about 3 a.m. when I finally crashed in the bus. About 7:30 a.m., the sun was beating in the windows, and the stale smell of beer woke me. I stumbled out to see what looked like some old Civil War scene, minus the Harleys. A fog-covered campground, bodies laying around, the campfire almost out, a few people walking around in a daze, and the sound of snoring. It was like a movie, but we were living it instead of just watching it.

CHAPTER 2

THE TWIG IS BENT

I've been asked why I am like I am, but I really don't have a clue. As a kid, when I acted up, I was disciplined like most of the kids of my era—spare the rod, spoil the child—and whenever I was caught, I knew what the outcome would be. I never took it personal. You either learned to behave or got better at what you were doing.

Some would say it could be because of my IQ (145, of which I probably left a chunk behind during the '60s), and growing up in the '50s, there were no special school programs. So I became bored easily. All I know is, what I did just seemed to come naturally to me, like breathing.

I really do wonder to this day, though, about my actions as a child. I was brought up by honest and loving parents, but it seemed like I was a bad seed. The only thing I can figure out is I must have had something left over from a former life. Maybe I was a highwayman or an outlaw—who knows? To this day I can't wear anything tight around my neck, like my body had a memory of being hung or having my head cut off. Even when my mother died in 2005 and I had to wear a suit to the funeral, I tied the tie real loose around my neck.

I don't remember much about my early childhood on the East Side of Saint Paul. I was the oldest kid in a family of nine—first four boys and then five girls. My folks both worked to support us, and then after my dad died when he was forty-two, my mom kept on working. My grandma Goldie used to babysit us early on.

Probably the first thing I remember was the gas tank incident. I was about five years old. We lived in an old house on the corner where Front, Como, and Dale Streets all come together. I was always on the go, exploring all the garages and buildings around us whenever I could get away. As they used to say, if you blinked, I was gone.

One day when I had snuck out while Grandma was watching my brothers, another little boy from the neighborhood got hit by a car at the crossing about two houses down. I didn't see it—I was already too far away—but I learned about it afterward. He had dark hair like me, and everyone thought it *was* me. So they contacted my parents, and they went down to the hospital with everyone else, expecting to see their son dead. (There had been a lot of blood in the street.) Only it wasn't me after all.

That set off a massive search for me, to which I was oblivious at the time because I had discovered a lake three blocks away and decided to explore it. It was about as big as a football field. As I was checking it out, I found an old gas tank bobbing against the shore. I figured it was my own personal yacht and set out with a stick for a paddle.

Meanwhile one of my playmates had told my parents where I was, and they all took off to retrieve their prodigal son. When they got there, I was going back and forth across

the lake having a ball. Mom, Dad, and Grandma coaxed me off the lake by holding out a candy bar, probably a 7-Up, my favorite, but I don't remember. I do remember feeling something like dread when I paddled up to the shore, but they met me with hugs and kisses for the son that they had thought was lost to them.

After the joy of the moment had passed and I was home behind closed doors, though, I had my second paddling experience of the day. I got whopped so hard that they had to keep me inside for about two weeks until the bruises didn't show anymore.

The next house we lived in was a little nicer place in the suburb of Maplewood. I was about seven when we moved. I was always a very inquisitive child, and in this neighborhood I started exploring other people's garages and houses and finding things that interested me. (This was what the older people called burglary.)

My first real burglary was when I was still almost seven. We had a neighbor couple that my parents visited quite often, a real Ozzie and Harriet type. They had a nice little rambler with one room fixed up for all his Army souvenirs from World War II, including a BAR machine gun. This really grabbed my attention when I first saw it. Wow! What a great gun to play Army with!

Well, that thought stayed in my mind, and I took several trips over to see the gun when my neighbors were home. They were always happy to see me and let me in. Then one day I went over to look at the gun, but no one was home. However, the back door was open, so I let myself in and went to that special room. There was the gun just waiting for me. I figured I might just borrow it for a while to show my friends, so I picked it up and took it.

What I didn't realize was how heavy that gun was. It was almost as big as I was, and I was a big kid—more than four feet tall already. But I was not to be put off, and I lugged it home in broad daylight. How I managed to do that—carry a machine gun down a city street without anyone saying "What the hell is going on?" is still a mystery to me. The gun must have weighed half as much as I did, but I was determined to have it.

As soon as I got it home and dragged it to the room I shared with Billy, my brother, my folks came home from work. I was there thinking I had the world's neatest gun to play Army with when my mother came in. She yelled for my father, and no amount of storytelling could save me. My parents took me and the gun (my dad carried it this time) back to the neighbors—who were home now—and apologized for my transgression. The neighbors informed us that I was no longer welcome around their house, and with that my parents' visits ceased, too.

Back in Maplewood, the episode with the machine gun wasn't the only trouble I got into. Because I was the oldest kid, I was always on the lookout for adventure. I got away with stuff, too, partly because I was what I guess you'd call a cute little shit with dark hair and big brown eyes. My brother Billy was two years younger with blond hair. Although he was small for his age, he was my partner in crime because he followed me everywhere and did what I said.

One day, though, I got away by myself. Our babysitter this time was a big woman, a distant cousin, who spent the day sitting on our couch, eating and watching TV. She didn't pay much attention to us, which was not a good thing. This time when I snuck out, I headed for one of the garages across the street. All the houses and garages were pretty much the same, and since I'd been through the garages before, I knew they mostly held tools, lawnmowers, and camping equipment. This was familiar territory for me.

One garage, though, held a surprise. I had climbed up off the floor into the rafters, and I found a box full of photographs of things I'd never seen before. The people in them—they were the neighbors who lived there—had no clothes on, and they were doing some funny stuff. I found all this quite interesting, so I climbed down with the pictures in my hands and went out to show them to all my playmates, who were quite interested, too. I don't remember exactly, but I think I sold a few to the kids who had money.

Well, within days, one of the parents got hold of one of the pictures, and all of us were rounded up. The pictures we could find were given back to the proper owners, and none of the kids were allowed to play with me anymore. I spent most of the summer indoors, grounded, or at least I was supposed to be.

The funny thing is, when I was about twenty-two, I was working at Gould Battery, a company in Saint Paul. A bunch of us guys, wearing our nametags, were hanging around the time clock waiting to punch out. A lady who worked there too came up, looked at my nametag, and turned white. "Did you ever live in Maplewood on Eldridge when you were little?" she asked.

"Yeah," I said.

She looked at me like I was shit. "You were an *evil little kid,*" she said, and turned away.

As it happened, she was the lady who had owned the garage with the pictures. She managed to avoid me the rest of the time I worked at Gould's, and she never spoke to me again.

CHAPTER 3

SCHOOL WARS

One of the first school experiences I remember is when I was in second grade. We were still living on Eldridge in Maplewood, and I was going to Presentation of the Blessed Virgin Mary on Larpenteur. I rode the bus to and from school, and the bus stop was right across the street from my house. So, even though it was the middle of winter, I wore just a spring baseball jacket this day, one of those cotton ones with the bases on the back.

Well, for some reason I was kept after school and I missed my bus. Back then we didn't have wind chills, but it was as cold as hell. I had to walk home carrying my books and lunch box, a Heckel and Jeckel one, so I started out. I remembered the way because of the bus ride, but I didn't have to stop at all the corners. After about two blocks, I dropped all my books, and the lunch box lasted only about another block. My hands were really cold, so cold that I didn't care about the trouble I could get into about losing the books—I just wanted to get my hands warm in my pockets.

As I trudged on, I had no idea that my not getting off my regular bus at the corner had caused such a stir. My mother had called the school and found out I was kept after. When they couldn't find me, they learned from the nun who kept me after that I was walking home.

This news sent everyone into a panic because it was below zero and I wasn't dressed for such an adventure. The cops were called, and my mother tried to get ahold of my father at work. She was in a frenzy. She didn't drive, so she went to a neighbor and got her to drive up to the school so she could look for me. The cops were out looking, too—after all, it shouldn't be so hard to find a little brown-haired boy in a red summer jacket with no hat or gloves.

I would probably have been found right away if I'd stayed on the road, but when I got by Wakefield Lake, I went cross-country to save some time and get warm as fast as I could. I remember falling several times because of the deep snow, but I kept going. I finally made it to Frost Avenue, and I knew it was only about eight more blocks to home, but I was freezing. I made a game out of it the best I could, though, pretending I was a soldier and I had duties to perform. I wanted to be tough like my dad, who was a paratrooper and sergeant at age sixteen in Italy during World War II. I didn't want to fail.

I still remember how cold my feet were—they felt like cold bricks. (I still have trouble with them in cold weather.) But I kept on. When I got about six blocks from my house, a neighbor I didn't recognize saw me, stopped, and tried to get me into his car. But no way—I wasn't supposed to talk to strangers, and I didn't. What a time to actually do what I was told!

Well, the neighbor went right to my house and said he had seen me over on Frost by Gladstone School. By then my dad was home, and he took off to get me. I was never so happy to see him as when he pulled up, jumped out of the

car, grabbed me, and gave me a big hug that would have probably hurt if I wasn't so numb.

After I got home and warmed up, my parents really raised hell with the school, and I was never kept after again.

Several years later, we moved to the Mount Airy project after my dad was hurt in a construction accident. I transferred to St. Mary's on Ninth Street in Saint Paul and walked to school through what is now I-94. We used to stop at the old Mississippi Market and throw rocks at the rats that were in the trash. There was a store there, and St. Mary's was just two blocks from the Farmers Market (which was a parking lot during the week) and four blocks from the Emporium and all the downtown stores.

I started off right away in trouble. I used to have a real problem with morning Mass, which we had to attend every day. I was always real uncomfortable, and I mean *real uncomfortable*. I would try to ditch, and once I even tried to fake fainting, and it drove the nuns crazy. I was always in the office getting disciplined (or should I say getting the shit beat out of my hands with a pointer or ruler—I am surprised they still work). Besides the Mass incidents, I was always screwing around, like the time I stole a bunch of Ex-Lax and gave it to the kids on the playground.

Every chance I got, I would ditch school. It just seemed too boring. I would go to the public library to read and listen to classical music, even when I was real little. You had your own little room to listen in, and it was great. I was reading Shakespeare and lots of other stuff (*Hamlet* was one of my favorites)—I think the nuns were glad not to have me around. All except Sister St. Peter, the one I had in seventh grade. She was really nice, and when she found out I was reading Shakespeare and could comprehend it, she would sit and talk to me about it.

Besides going to the library, I would go on shopping adventures at all the downtown stores—the Emporium, Donaldsons, T. W. Grant, and the like. I could steal anything that wasn't nailed down, and even some things that were. I guess it was partly because I was such a cute kid with the big brown eyes, dark hair, and a smile that would melt a lot of hearts (or so I've been told). And when I wasn't in the stores, I was going through the cars parked in Farmers Market for whatever I could find.

This went on for quite a while until, when I was thirteen, I picked up a pair of binoculars at Donaldsons. They cost about $70, which was a lot back then. Well, my mom caught me with them, and I couldn't convince her that a friend had borrowed them to me. She took me to see the priest, who took me to the principal, but all she did was check my locker. It was full of troll dolls, baseballs, pen-and-pencil sets, several baseball gloves, and other trinkets. They decided that I was not St. Mary's material, and I was expelled. To this day, I swear I remember one of the nuns telling my mother they thought I was the Antichrist.

What my mother did was take everything from the locker, and off we went, binoculars and all. The first stop was the Emporium and the security office. They figured out what was from their store, took my picture for their records, and informed me I was no longer welcome there. I remember the man behind the desk asking me all these questions, and when he asked me if I had any aliases, I didn't know what he was talking about. Then he told me that *alias* meant a name you were called besides your real name. I answered

his question by saying, "Yeah, Tank," because I was good in football and that's what they called me there.

My mother cuffed me on the head and said, "Don't be so cocky." Then the scene was replayed at several other stores, and my shopping days were over.

Shortly after that, I started at Franklin School, which was across from the Farmers Market. It was a public school and had a totally different student body. These were the rough kids, not the nicey-nice kids in Catholic school, and they thought, Oh, looky here, a nicey-nice Catholic school kid—let's have fun. Well, the next day I got detention for some reason, and there I was in my own little breakfast club. I started out okay, but then the teacher left the room and the taunting and paper throwing began.

"Knock it off," I said, and then this mulatto kid named Kenny came up and started picking on me and trying to go through my pockets. Before I knew it, he was getting his ass kicked by some other kids, and that was the start of my friendship with Pat O'Leary and Darrell Bennett, two kids in detention who decided I would make a good addition to their little clique. I even ran into one of my first cousins, Bobby Hayes, my uncle Howie's kid. He lived in the projects, too, and we became really tight.

I was always in trouble for screwing around and got the normal punishments like detention or having to stand in front of the class holding a dictionary in each hand with my arms stretched out. That sucked at first, but I got pretty good at it. This one teacher. Mr. Smith, was a real piece of shit, always belittling everyone. He had all the girls seated in the first two rows, and he must have had bad hands because he was always dropping shit like pens and pencils and bending over to pick them up. (Even I figured that one out.)

Anyway, one time me and my cousin Bobby were screwing around in his class, and he called us up to the front. I figured, Great, the dictionaries again, but then he told Bobby to bend over, and he took out this huge paddle with all these holes drilled in it, and SMACK! he whacked Bobby on the ass. I mean, it made my butt pucker. Then he looked at me and said, "Bend over."

Well, out came "In your dreams!" No way was I going to take this shit—after all, I was in the eighth grade, about five-foot-ten, 165, and the only person I was afraid of was my dad.

Off we went to the principal's office, my dad was called, and down he came. He was not happy. But when the teacher told him what had transpired, my dad said, "If anyone lays a hand on my son, I'll knock the living shit out of that person. If there's a problem, tell me and I'll take care of it."

As we were walking away, I was feeling pretty cocky. Then, out of nowhere came the smack on the back of my head that let me know all was not well, and I better straighten up.

About a week after all of this, report cards were going to come out, and Bobby, me, and Doug thought it would be fun to break into the school and take them. I said we should take them all, not just ours, because otherwise they'd know who it was. Then that night we met at the Mount Airy playground. None of us really knew what we were doing, but you have to start somewhere. I remember how scared I was, but at the same time I was almost high from the excitement.

When we got to the school, we found an open window and in we went. The sensation I got standing there in the dark was like nothing I had ever felt. My heart was pounding and I could hear the blood flowing in my ears. My palms

were sweaty, my skin felt like it was electric, and I was scared shitless, but I didn't want to be anywhere else. That was my first experience with what people call the "juice." It's better than food, drugs, sex—it's unbelievable. Wow.

We went through the rooms and got the report cards, and even found some money in the office—a little bonus. Then we left, threw away the report cards, and headed to White Castle to spend our ill-gotten gains on burgers and fries.

The next day the police were all over trying to figure out who did this. Even though I was really scared, I wouldn't have changed a thing. Not knowing whether we would get away with it was just as fun as the actual burglary. They never found out either.

Mr. Smith still kept on my case since the paddle incident. I mean, he went way out of his way to make my life miserable, and this went on for several months even after the burglary. When it was getting close to graduation time (from eighth grade—I was still only thirteen), I decided I'd had my fill. I found out what car was his—an old VW—and during the lunch hour I set it on fire. I had to get back for all those elbows and way-over-the-top blocks during football games that he took part in on the playground. I guess he thought he was going to get away with it, but I remembered every black-and-blue mark. I think he had some idea who the arsonist was, but he never said a word to me.

After graduating from Franklin, I went to Mechanic Arts for ninth grade. The first day I went to the office to get a class switched, and this black kid was there getting pretty smart with the assistant principal. They took him in, the door slammed shut, and I heard a lot of commotion. When he came out, he was nowhere near as smart as before, and I decided then and there to keep my nose clean.

Pretty soon I was doing quite well in school—I even joined the band. I was also the first freshman to be allowed to join Junior Achievement. I really got into science, and I was a real nerd with the Buddy Holly glasses, pocket protector, and three of my own microscopes with slide collections. But I was also the nerd who would kick your ass if you messed with him or with someone who couldn't stand up for himself.

But my activities went beyond science. I had become adept at breaking and entering. Me and several of my friends always had quarters, and I mean lots of quarters. Laundromats were abundant, and I got real good at using a pick, so we were never broke.

Halfway through ninth grade, we moved to Cottage Grove southeast of Saint Paul, and I started in at Oltman Junior High. After Mechanic Arts, this was like preschool. The kids didn't have a clue, even the bad ones. No one even knew what pot was, and I found that to my advantage. I sold a lot of oregano and even had regular customers. I also got off on the wrong foot with the principal, Mr. Corless. My long hair and bell-bottom pants with the Beatle boots and their horseshoe cleats made me stand out like a rat turd in a bag of rice.

I also started to hang around with the Mexicans or the wannabe Mexicans—that Baldy and Greaser thing was going on at the time. One day I was out talking to my new friend, Dickie Costello, and these two kids came up, one white and one Mexican. Jimmy Jam, the white guy, thought I was messing with Dickie, and he said, "I'm gonna tab you, you mutterpucker."

I said, "What?!"

"I'm gonna tab you, you mutterpucker," he said again.

I looked at Dickie and asked, "What the hell is he saying?"

Dickie laughed and said, "He's going to stab you, you motherf***er." (The kid had a speech defect, but I didn't know that.)

Then Jimmy Jam pulled out a knife from his jacket, a metallic green one that was big with the greasers. Dick said, "No, he's all right, he's with us."

The first fight I saw was out on the football field. A bunch of people were there watching while the two guys sat for at least five minutes saying, "You hit me first," and then, "No, you hit *me* first." Finally a few punches were thrown and everyone was buddies again. I'd seen girl fights in the projects that were 100 percent better than that—no "you hit me" shit. If someone was taking off her coat, the other one was all over her. And the guy fights—man, I mean sticks, rocks, bottles, chairs, and even a three-foot piece of garden hose. When it was over, both were bloody, and one of them was really tore up.

I finally got into my first fight—I think he was about to start that "you hit me" shit, and I knocked him out. After several fights, that you-first shit stopped. It didn't take long before I was that kid who no one's parents would let their kid hang out with. That was okay, though, because what teenage girl listens to her parents? It got even better after I was shot the first time.

I got into the standard trouble in high school—ditching, fighting, drinking, and blowing up the toilet with M-80s (which I actually didn't do but got blamed for anyway). But in my sophomore year I got in a fight in the parking lot with a senior who had snowballed my little brother, who was about twelve, and then smashed my brother's face into the snow. Now, I can do that, but not anyone else. I went to this kid's house, and he stood there behind a closed door, making faces at me and giving me the finger. I just left, and then several days later I ran into him with several friends in the parking lot at school. They thought, Who is this sophomore who thinks he can just come up to us without being summoned? Well, I showed them as I strolled up and slammed this guy in the jaw with a left hook. Everyone took off when they saw all the blood, so I figured I made my point, and off to German I went.

About twenty minutes into class, the principal and two cops showed up to take me out of class. I ended up getting expelled, went to court, and had to pay $500 to the kid whose jaw I broke. I had no idea how bad it was until I saw the scar on the side of his face. Funny, about five years later I was hitchhiking on Highway 61, and this same kid picked me up. We had a real good talk about it all. He still had the scar. That was it for high school. I got my GED later, but that's another story.

CHAPTER 4

HOW I GOT MY NAME

One thing I can say with certainty is that I have not had a dull life. I have been shot twice, stabbed, blown up, bitten by a rattlesnake and by a scorpion, plus survived numerous car and motorcycle accidents. Then there've been a lot of other things I both can and can't remember. If being married twice counts, I've been there, too.

When I was sixteen, I was shot for the first time. I had snuck out of the house to hang around with some kids from school, and one of them, Bob, had a 22-caliber pellet pistol that looked like a Ruger. So we went target shooting in his basement, using BBs to hit pop cans. When we got bored, Rick said, "Let's go over to my house and check out the models I've built," and off we went.

When we got there, we went up to his room. His parents were downstairs watching TV. Bob still had the gun, and he started playing around with it. He figured it was empty, so he pointed it at my face and pulled the trigger. I felt a puff of wind and yelled to knock it off—and then all of a sudden I felt a pain in my left eye. I hurried into the bathroom, looked in the mirror, and saw that the white part of my left eye had turned red. When I covered my right eye with my hand, I couldn't see a thing.

After that, I started to panic. I burst back into the room, took the gun from Bob, and shook it. Some BBs rattled around inside. "I thought it was empty!" he yelled. "I just wanted to scare you!"

Back I went to the bathroom mirror. This time I noticed a small hole in my left eyelid. I was overcome with a feeling of dread. Why had I snuck out of the house to begin with? Why hadn't I listened for once? Now here I was with a BB in my head somewhere. This was something I couldn't talk myself out of like I usually did.

I went back in with Rick and Bob, who were freaking out about the trouble they were in. Rick told me to go home and it would get better. I thought, Yeah, better for them—they're probably hoping I'll die in my sleep so they'll be off the hook. But I had enough sense to say I had to go to the hospital and that we had to tell Rick's dad.

So we did that, and when he took one look at my eye, we were off to the Emergency Room at Mounds Park. I just kept thinking that I was going to die, only sixteen and on my way out, and I should have listened to my parents. Rick's dad kept saying, "Are you all right? Stay awake. Keep talking." He must have been as scared as I was.

At the ER, they whisked me off to the exam room and then to X-ray. It all seemed so dreamlike that I wasn't scared anymore. Back in the exam room, I heard the nurse call for an eye specialist and a neurosurgeon, but what really upset me was when she called my folks and told them to get down to the hospital because their son had been shot. I felt so sick at what I was putting them through—I just wanted to tell

them how sorry I was and that they shouldn't worry because everything would be okay.

I was kind of drifting in and out and then there was my mom bending down and kissing me. The last thing I remember was her whispering, "Don't tell any of your Asian jokes because your doctor is Asian!" I wasn't in any shape for a comedy routine, but she knew me pretty well.

After several days, I came to in a room upstairs with both my eyes bandaged, and I freaked out. Luckily a nurse was there, and she told me I wasn't blind, but that I had to keep my eyes (and myself) quiet because the BB had shattered inside my head close to my brain. If I didn't move, they figured that flesh would grow around the fragments and I wouldn't be in danger anymore. So I had to spend a month and a half killing time, blind in a hospital room, but at least I ended up with no brain damage.

While I was in the hospital, every single day during the week, my mother left her work at 3 p.m. and walked nine blocks in the dead of winter to get me coneys, hoagies, or something else that I liked to eat. Then she'd come by bus to visit me, watch me eat, and take the bus home to care for everyone else. Despite all this, I just couldn't help playing a joke on her one time when she brought coneys. I ate them while she was visiting, and just then they brought my regular dinner. I said, "Mom, why don't you have some of it if you want?" So she was eating some soup and drinking the juice when a nurse came in. I couldn't help it—as the nurse got near my bed, I said, sounding groggy, "Mom, did they bring my food? I'm really hungry." There she was eating it while the nurse gave her this weird look (as I found out later). My mom was so embarrassed.

I got awfully bored during all that time in the hospital. But I was lucky—several of the nurses used to read to me, and I got this image of what they looked like from their voices. (Not even close.) I listened to the radio a lot—I still hate the song "Michelle." It seemed like it played every ten minutes. When the doctors took the bandages off, I still had to wait a week before I could go home, but I was sure glad to go there when they let me.

Only once I was home, I had some problems, too. I was like a little kid who didn't want to be in the dark, so I had to have the lights on at night or I couldn't sleep. And then on my second day home, Cottage Grove's finest showed up looking for me. Evidently a church had been broken into and they had some eyewitness who said it was me.

Since I'd gotten shot on January 6 and spent seven weeks in the hospital, and the burglary took place January 20, you'd have thought that they'd have said, "Sorry," and left. But even though I'd been strapped down to a hospital bed with my eyes bandaged at the time, they ignored my parents' pleas and my own protests and dragged me off to jail. I didn't have the best reputation, but there was no way I could have done it. I was freaking out, swearing and yelling. My father finally convinced one of the officers to call the hospital, who confirmed my whereabouts on the 20th, and they let me go.

I'll tell you one thing—getting used to being blind in my left eye was a real bitch. Just the trauma was a shock. Driving was a challenge because my depth perception was gone. The surgeons had left my left eye in for cosmetic purposes, but that lasted only about four years because I used to get into a lot of fights and everyone always seemed to hit

me in that eye. This made me hemorrhage—talk about pain! Normal pressure in an eye is 12, and mine would go up into the 40s, which really sucked.

Finally the doctors had to remove my eye because it had atrophied so much that it really looked bad. The surgery was hard on me because the anesthetic didn't work right. I ended up nearly dying, and they had to beat on my chest to get my heart going again. One and a half hours, which was how long it was supposed to last, turned into almost four hours, while my mom and Edie (who I was married to at the time) sat in the waiting room. After it was all over, I was black and blue for a week.

Afterward, they gave me a prosthetic eye, which was a regular brown to match my right. But when I got my second prosthetic eye, I had it made white with a Harley bar and shield. Then I had one made with a smiley face, one with a hand giving the finger, and one that was bright blue.

I remember the fun I had with my fake eye, taking it out and dropping it in people's drinks in bars—until someone almost swallowed it. Like they say, it's funny until someone loses an eye. One time I went to the washroom after I'd told this girl I wanted to keep my eye on her, and I put it on the table. And then once I went out riding with the Los Valientes, and afterward some of the guys were shooting pool with some marines. I put my eye on the table and told them I wanted to see what was going on while I went to get a drink. By the time I came back, there was a fake leg, a hairpiece, a set of false teeth, and a fake boob on the table next to it. We could have almost built another person.

But after ten years I couldn't wear a prosthetic eye anymore because the socket was so damaged because of my fighting. I would have had to go through surgery again—no way. So now I have a permanent wink.

I guess it bothers a lot of people when they lose a body part, but you have to accept it. If you don't, you just get too caught up in it and never learn to adapt and realize there's nothing you can do to change it. You just have to move on.

CHAPTER 5

SHOT, SNAKE BIT, BLOWN UP, STABBED, AND STILL HERE

The second time I got shot was almost a year to the day after the first time, on January 9, 1967. I was at a party with about forty other people at this house on the west side of Cottage Grove. The kid's parents were on vacation, so he was going crazy—booze everywhere. We were sitting around drinking and watching this guy fighting with his girlfriend. After about twenty minutes, he hit her. I walked over to him, saying, "We're getting sick of this shit—knock it off."

He said, "I'm sorry, everything's cool."

And I said, "Okay."

But when I turned to go back into the kitchen, I felt a sharp pain in my lower right back. The music was so loud that I never heard the shot and thought he'd stabbed me. Before anyone could stop him, he took off as fast as he could, leaving his girlfriend behind. As fast as I could, I took off my leather jacket. When I pulled up my shirt, I could see a small hole with blood coming out. All hell broke loose—someone yelled, "He's shot," and there was a stampede for the door.

Two of my friends stuck by me, bent me over the counter,

and examined the wound. Dean said he could see something inside. Then someone else came up with a needle-nose pliers from somewhere, and before I knew it, they poured Jack Daniel's on the hole and pulled out the bullet with the pliers. I was lucky because I'd been wearing a biker-style leather jacket, and the bullet, which was only a 25-caliber, had to go through that first before it got into me.

The JD hurt more than the bullet did, and after my friends had bandaged me up, we set off to find the guy with the gun. We couldn't find him, but we located his girlfriend, and she said he'd gone back to Texas or Mexico or wherever the hell he came from. In the end, my parents never even knew what happened, and I healed great. I guess no matter what you do, your guardian angel still hangs around.

When I got bit by the rattlesnake, I was still a kid, about ten years old. I was hiking with this group who took kids at risk out camping for two weeks. (No surprise I was part of it.) I knew a lot of the guys at the drop-off point, but after the bus finally came, the ride was brutal. If I never hear "Ninety-Nine Bottles of Beer on the Wall" again, it will be too soon.

After what seemed like an eternity, we arrived at camp. When we got off the bus, we got put in big green tents, eight boys to a tent—I think the tents came from the army. I was with six kids I knew. It was the normal camping experience with hiking, crafts, canoeing, and crappy food. On the second night we snuck out to explore on our own and found the girls' cabin, so we did a little bird-watching. Then we discovered a supply cabin, which we accessed by climbing up under the carport—not that there was anything inside worth taking, but it was just the thrill of being somewhere you weren't supposed to be.

After about a week of the great outdoors, we were on a walk catching frogs and snakes, which is something boys just do naturally. I pulled up a rock and found this big snake about three feet long. I made a grab for it, and before I knew it, I had six tiny holes in my left hand but the snake in my right. The counselor came running up and saw me with one hand bleeding and a timber rattler in the other. He yelled, "Drop that snake!" which scared the living shit out of me, but I thought, No way, this sucker is mine. I finally did what the counselor wanted, though, and he chopped it in two pieces with a shovel.

So with the pieces of the snake and me both in the car, he tore off to the local hospital. They gave me some shots and cleaned and bandaged my hand, then kept me overnight so they could watch me. I guess they thought I might drop over, but the only thing that happened was my hand swelled up. Later that night, one of the doctors said he'd heard that sometimes when snakes bite humans, they don't inject venom but just save it for when they're hunting.

That sounded good to me, but I thanked my guardian angel again. By now I figured he should be getting hazard pay for being stuck with me.

The time I nearly got blown up, I was about fifteen, and of course it was the Fourth of July. The dad of one of the boys I hung out with had this shitload of machine gun shells, and we decided it was the thing to do, given the date and all, to take them apart and make a bomb. We took a one-quart beer bottle, filled it with gunpowder, and made a fuse out of masking tape and some more gunpowder. We found a field to try out our super-cracker, and somehow I ended up being the one to light it. As I was walking out, Rick grabbed it and said he should do it because the gunpowder was his dad's. He was about twenty feet ahead of me bending down with the match when the world lit up, and I was blown about twenty feet back.

Everything seemed in slow motion—the windows blowing out in the houses across the street, the car windows shattering, and Rick with his clothes shredded and blood everywhere. He managed to run home, though, and his mother, who was a nurse, took him to the hospital. I ran home, too, cleaned up, and waited. Sure as shit, the cops showed up at my door and started asking all these questions. I said, "I don't know nothing about it," and after a while they gave up.

Rick finally got out of the hospital. We couldn't believe he hadn't lost an eye or something, but he was okay except for tons of little scars. It was really a miracle, and it almost had happened to me. I was lucky that time.

Then there was the time I got stabbed in my stomach. I had gone over to talk to this guy who was going out with a friend's sister and was abusive to her. I'd had a talk with him several months before, and I thought he'd gotten the drift—no hitting on Amy—but I guess he had a short memory. (He'd been very agreeable then when I'd told him that when you get that mad, it's better to walk away and not have to be sorry for any words or actions that happen in the heat of the moment.) And here I was saying the same thing again, but this time my tone was a little stronger. He was just a little shit, and hitting him wouldn't be right, but I had him backed up against the wall. I heard a noise and turned to see what it was, when all of a sudden I felt this sharp pain in my stomach and looked down to see a Gerber survival knife sticking out of me. He just stood there with this shit-eating grin. I pulled out the knife—it had gone in about five

inches—and before I knew it, I had beat him into a bloody pulp. I guess I just lost it.

Then I went back to the biker clubhouse (I was in the motorcycle club Los Valientes then) because I felt like shit. I walked in, and there was Mother Mick and several other guys. Mick said, "What's wrong? You're pale as a ghost." I showed him the stab wound, and he reached over and stuck his finger in the hole up to his second knuckle. There wasn't much blood, but he grabbed me and said, "You got to go to the ER." I thought if I slept a couple of hours I would be okay, but no such luck.

When I got to the ER, they took me right in. The doctor checked out and cleaned the wound—he was amazed that there was no organ damage. The knife just went in and slipped by everything without a nick. After several hours and three doctors, I was packed up and sent home. The funny thing is, the guy who stabbed me was about three rooms over in the ER, and they kept him for ten days. He never said a word about who did that to him, and I said nothing about knowing who stabbed me. It was a push.

Another adventure was when I got stung by a scorpion. I was down in Texas with some people I knew, and we were out partying in the desert. There were about forty of us, mostly on bikes, and we'd been at it for three days. I'd slept in my tent for about four hours when I got up and started to put my boots on. Then I felt this shooting pain in my right heel. I mean, I thought someone had put a hot needle in my boot. I kicked it off, and as it hit the ground, out crawled this black scorpion. I yelled, and several people came over to see what the commotion was. By then I had my sock off, and my heel was red and swollen. Someone stamped on the scorpion. I said, "Are those poisonous?" and there was a general consensus that the red ones were but not the black ones. My friend Slow Hand said it didn't make much difference because we were about one and a half hours away from any medical help.

It's funny how you can think yourself into anything. After about fifteen minutes, I started to get dizzy and sweaty, and I got the shakes. Several people told me how pale I looked, and they figured we should just start for the hospital, so if I died, at least we'd be heading the right way. I jumped in the back of someone's pickup on several sleeping bags while everyone assured me things would be okay. It was a long, hot, dusty, bumpy ride, but we finally got to a clinic. My foot was swollen and my calf was throbbing. They looked at it—cleaned it out and bandaged it—and told me it wasn't poisonous or I would have been dead already. I was relieved.

I hobbled around for about a week, but my foot finally got back into shape. I tell you one thing—to this day I still shake my boots out whenever I put them on.

CHAPTER 6

PURPLE HAZE DAYS

If I remember right, my first experience with any mind-altering substance was when I was about fourteen. Several friends in the Mount Airy project where I lived at the time introduced me to pot. It was okay, but since I didn't smoke cigarettes, it never really caught on for me.

I think it was 1963 or '64 when my family moved to Cottage Grove that I made new friends and introduced them to my old friends, and the party was on. I got my first taste of alcohol around then—someone had a bottle of Four Roses, and I knew I had another new friend. From the start it was balls to the wall drinking for me, to the point of passing out. I would be the life of the party, telling stories and jokes. People would come just because I was there. I didn't have a fear after two drinks, which always consisted of a Welch's Grape Jelly glass half full of straight booze. I kept the same glass from my first drink throughout the next year—it was my magic glass, it made me popular and happy.

In my first several years of drinking, I can honestly say I never drank without passing out. I got to be quite the legend for my antics, passing out and falling down stairs or out a window or two, but I finally learned when the end was near because my lips would start to go numb. Then I would look for a safe place to pass out.

When I think back, I can't believe how easy it was to get alcohol. I even started buying it when I was eighteen because I looked older. Everyone could get as much as he wanted without even trying too hard.

The drug use really started shortly after I got shot the first time when I was sixteen. I was in the hospital, and I was waiting to call a girl I knew. The nurse gave me a sleeping pill, and I fought it, but wow, what a feeling! I was relaxed and felt great. I made my call, and Donna asked me what was up because I sounded too happy for a guy who was in the hospital with a pellet in his head.

Well, the next day I found out what the pills were and made a note, because when I left the hospital I figured I was going to need some of them for my sleeping problem (or any other problem). When I got home, there were my sleeping pills—Seconals (reds)—and my old friend whiskey had a new buddy. I was quick to learn about all the little pills that brightened my world—reds, tewies, 747s, and lots more. If I had a dollar for every time my face hit a coffee table after nodding off, I would be at least a thousandaire.

Pretty soon along came 1967 and, boy oh boy, you talk about drugs! The first time I took acid I was at a party on the East Side of Saint Paul at a commune there. There were several cases of Boone's Farm Apple wine, so I grabbed a bottle, and then someone gave me a small paper and said to drop it in the wine. It was Orange Sunshine, and that was my first bottle of electric wine. That's about all I remembered until three days later.

I figured I had to get to know about this acid because we were going to spend a lot of time together. I actually got

quite good at tripping and always figured on at least three days because I was serious. It was the commune era, too, and I moved into my first one the summer of 1967. I thought I'd died and went to heaven—booze, drugs, and all the sex I could handle. After all, we were the love generation.

I remember our first commune on Dayton Avenue. It was a six-plex, and I lived in the closet under the front room stairs. It was great—pillows, black light with posters, and I could trip without anyone messing with me. The acid back then was unreal—you could trip for days. It was nothing to be talking to someone and see the words coming out of their mouth, or something would be growing out of their head. You learned how to control it after a while, but sometimes you had a bad trip anyway and freaked out. Sometimes I just used to say, "It's only a movie, only a movie" to hold myself together. The sex was great when you were on acid—sometimes you would melt into each other's bodies, and you could go on for hours—or so we thought.

It was about December in 1967 when I first shot acid. I was at a party in Minneapolis, and several other stoners were sitting there listening to Jefferson Airplane. Out came some acid, and someone took out several needles. As I watched, they put a torn-up cigarette filter on a spoon, dropped some water and some coke in it, and fired it up. I was mesmerized but had no interest in the coke—I didn't want to be wired any more than I already was. Then Brian asked me if I liked acid, and I said, "Sure." I told him I had dropped it and peeked it (that's when you drop it into your eye—since I had one that was bad already, no harm—and it hits you right away).

Then someone said, "You got to try to shoot it," and I thought, Okay.

Well, as I waited and they fixed it, my heart was racing

and I started to sweat like crazy. I was really nervous. Then they tied a rubber tube around my arm about mid-bicep, and I waited some more. I can still remember the first poke of the needle and how scared I was, but what was there to lose? I felt this pressure in my vein, and then, as they untied the tube, it was like the Star Wars movies when you go into warp speed. The world exploded—I was bombarded with sights, sound, and feelings. Trying to tell someone what it's like is like trying to explain an orgasm to a virgin. You just had to be there.

With all the acid I used to buy—I got Purple Haze by the hundreds—everyone thought I was dealing, but it was all for me.

All this drug use began to take a toll on me and my parents as well. My mother worked in downtown Saint Paul and would stumble over me on Seventh Street between Bridgeman's and Dayton's. I had been moving from commune to commune and finally settled in one at 830 Ashland with about twelve other people. We supported ourselves by panhandling and stealing. I was seventeen at the time, but this was just my normal life.

Like always, I ended up as the caretaker. One day started when I woke up to the sun shining in the shadeless window, and when I rolled over, I found someone from the night before. I wasn't sure who she was, but now I had something to do with that morning wood. After several friendly pokes, she and I were of the same mind and lived up to that love generation tag. Then we wandered into the kitchen to get some nourishment, and there was Danny and Bunny going through the cabinets, Danny saying how we needed to make a grocery run and Bunny complaining how there was hardly any food, just wine and drugs.

Now I always ate well because I was going out with several waitresses who worked at the lunch counters in stores downtown, and they always took good care of me. (I took good care of them, too, of course, in other ways.) We did most of our shopping at about 4 a.m. when the bakeries used to drop off the bakery items in big silver delivery boxes outside of the country club and Red Owl stores. Then we'd hit the milk delivery trucks that were parked for breakfast at the Spa on Seven Corners.

One of the other commune members came into the kitchen and said his well-off uncle was going out of town for some reason or another, and that he was a real jerk who thought he was better than everyone else in his family. I told them we should watch his house—it was in a real nice area of Highland Park. On Friday night we saw him put several bags in his car and leave, so we watched until it was really dark and then went to work. We went through the kitchen and the freezer in the basement until we were pretty well stocked up, especially with the contents of his liquor cabinet. We also got some bedding for several new arrivals.

We were just about ready to head out when the phone rang. What did I do?—I answered it. Someone asked for Dave, and I said, "Dave's not here." The guy asked if he could leave a message, and I said I wouldn't be here to give him the message. Then he asked who I was, and I said, "The burglar."

Well, he laughed and laughed and told me the message anyway. I've always wondered what the look on his face was like when he talked to Dave and said he'd left a message with some guy who said he was the burglar.

Somewhere along in here, I met this beautiful girl named

Pat. She and her friend Cindy were hanging around the Dayton's air door, and I knew I was in trouble when I saw her. She was about five-foot-eight with long black hair, beautiful brown eyes, and the cutest overbite. We ended up going out for several months, which was a long-term relationship back then. I still remember the last time we made love—it was at a friend's house on the pool table. She got pregnant, and back then the dad didn't have any say about things, especially if he was a seventeen-year-old hippie drug user whose only job was panhandling. So she put the baby, a girl, up for adoption. I never got a chance to see her, but there isn't a day I don't think about her. When I was older and dating a lot of younger women, I used to ask every new one exactly when she was born—I always had this fear that she might be my daughter. I just hope she had a better chance with someone other than me for a dad, and that she got her mother's beauty and brains.

I remember that right before I finally went straight, I was involved with some real freaks and ended up holding a psychedelic-painted mailbox full of coke. They'd gotten in trouble and gone out to Denver, so I was keeping the stash for them. I hid it in my parents' garage up in the rafters, but, as luck would have it, my dad and brothers decided to clean the garage and threw it out—only I didn't know that. When the guys came back and I couldn't find the box, they said I owed them $5,000, and when I said, "No way," they put out the word on the street that they'd give anybody the $5,000 who beat me up real bad.

That was a very bad year for me—there were at least a dozen attempts to collect. The closest they ever came was one time when I was partying in an old rundown hotel on

Wabasha where the cockroaches made a racket running for cover when you turned on the lights. I noticed this one guy giving me frog eyes, and I said, "What's your problem?"

"You're Purple Haze, right?" he said. (That was my nickname from the acid I used—and my last name was Hayes.) "There's a reward out for you," he added, and the fight was on.

It started out okay for me, but then it began to go his way, and I was wondering why my friends weren't coming to my aid. So I just yelled "Stop!" and he was so surprised that he did stop long enough for me to grab a lamp and hit him on the side of the head with it. He went down, and I pounded the piss out of him. Finally my friends pulled me off him, or I probably would have killed him.

The last I saw of this bunch was once when I was going out with Edie, my future first ex-wife. We were driving on the Loop in my '68 GTX, and this car with the two guys and three friends pulled up next to us, yelling that they were going to kill me. Edie was upset and so was I, but after a short car chase, we lost them. Several months later, I heard they got busted in another state on a robbery charge, so they and the reward were just a fond memory.

By the fall of 1969, this lifestyle started to lose its allure. Then in September, I was in a car accident. Lonnie and Terry, this married couple I'd been crashing with, and my pal Howie, decided to take Lonnie's '66 GTO out and teach Terry how to drive a stick. We were zipping around West Saint Paul and Eagan, and she was getting the hang of the four-speed, when she pulled into this driveway on Dodd Road and started to back out. The car killed, and we were blocking the westbound lane. As she was trying to start it, I saw several cars off in the distance coming our way and joked that we were going to get hit.

Well, the cars came closer and closer until the first one sped around us. But the second car nailed us dead-center on the driver's side doing about 50. We were pushed about forty feet sideways, and Terry was pushed into the passenger seat with Lonnie. Howie, who was sitting behind Terry, was pushed behind where I'd been sitting, and I ended up through the windshield, lying on the hood out cold. Everyone else walked away with bumps and minor cuts, but lucky me, the farthest away from the impact, ended up with a concussion, forty stitches in my head, and a dislocated shoulder. Go figure.

I was in the hospital for about a week, and I did some thinking. Pat and Cindy visited me, and that was the last time I saw Pat before she had our baby. I guess all that made me think that maybe I should reconsider my vocation—"hippie" didn't seem to have a lot of career advancement. Another life change was that I woke up craving orange pop and chow mein—two things I'd hated before the accident—and hating Mexican food. I mean, even the smell made me sick.

After I got out, I moved in with my parents and stopped using drugs. I still drank, but not to excess. In December of that year, I met my future first ex-wife, Edie, and stopped drinking, got a car, and remained clean and sober for seven years. Then one St. Patrick's Day I went out for corned beef and cabbage and was gone for three days. The first thing I remember is crawling up our alley behind York a half block off Arcade—I couldn't even remember where I'd parked my car, which took two days to find. I also found out I was 86'd from every bar on Arcade and Payne.

I always wonder why I started back drinking after being sober for so long. But my drinking continued, and I was back to the old me, balls to the wall. My tolerance had increased, and Edie was stuck shouldering the burden of the bills. If that wasn't bad enough, I had gotten back into motorcycles and joined the Spokesmen Motorcycle Club and fallen back into drug use with coke as my new choice because it made partying easier and longer.

Edie and I talk about this time, and all she really says is that I wasn't always such a nice guy, but I was what she was stuck with. I was the one who came out ahead on that deal.

CHAPTER 7

BIRTH OF AN OUTLAW

My relationship with motorcycles and motorcycle clubs began when I was about fourteen. I lived in Cottage Grove, and a lot of the kids I hung around with had small bikes—Honda 50s, Bridgestones, and even a Wizzer. Well, I told everyone I was going to get a Honda 50 Cub, and my parents ended up getting me one so I wouldn't look like a liar.

That was a great summer. I took off the faring from my bike and could get it up to 50 mph. We were supposed to ride only on the trails, but me being me, I was all over, including some trips to Minneapolis. I really had the fever for bikes, and I didn't get busted until around my birthday in August, because I was too young, had no license, etc., etc., etc. Oh well, that had to happen sooner or later. At least I wasn't drinking—I didn't drink when I was riding.

The following summer, I met a new friend, Tom Reed, at the Cook's Nook, a drive-in by my house. He was a couple of years older, and he had a Honda 305 Dream. Somehow I talked him into letting me ride it, and I took off. When I finally came back about three hours later, he was nowhere to be found, but when I went home he was sitting on my front steps. He was somewhat upset, but we became good friends anyway, and we did a lot of riding together.

That summer my parents let me buy a Suzuki X5 Invader with the money I made from my summer job laying sod, and off I went. That thing was really fast. During the time I had it, I hit everything I could, from a dog to a house. I went through two front ends, three front wheels, and one gas tank. I had to paint it several times, but it was great.

My next bike was a Harley 1949 Panhead Chopper. I remember because I was in junior high, and I could get a motorcycle license when I was fifteen. It was the only year you were allowed to get a motorcycle license before you could get a regular driver's license. When I rode the bike to school, I parked in the same lot as the teachers, causing quite a stir. The next year they made sure no student could ride or drive anything to school.

A break in my motorcycle interest came, though, after I was shot in January of 1966. I was drinking and using drugs seriously, and I stopped concentrating on bikes—probably a good thing. Then when I was twenty-eight and married to Edie and building cars for racing, I built this '65 Nova 327, 375-horsepower with a four-speed Muncey rock crusher. This guy showed up who wanted to buy it, but he wanted to give me part of the money and make up the rest with a Norton Commando Chopper. It had a rigid frame with an eight-inch over front end Sportster tank, sixteen-inch back wheel, and a king and queen seat. It was purple and white, and I was a biker again.

I rode that bike a couple of months, then sold it and picked up a Sportster. Edie didn't like bikes, so I did a lot of solo riding. One of the guys I worked with at Gould Battery rode with a club called the Spokesmen out of South Saint

Paul. They'd been around about fifteen years, and two of their members, Pitso and POA (Piece of Ass), asked me if I wanted to prospect after I'd been hanging around for a month or so. I said yes.

After that, I prospected for about a year, so they could get to know me and me them. It's like being a pledge to a fraternity but a lot more fun. Prospecting can be as easy or as hard as you made it. You always wanted to be sure you paid attention, had cigs, matches, rubbers, a sewing kit, shit like that, and you were the gofer and the yard man, bike washer, house cleaner, and general shit catcher.

The club members were always coming up with little tasks, like the time there were three prospects, including me, and it was the dead of winter, and Joe's truck didn't have heat, and Buttser came up with the idea that they wanted a pizza from this pizza place in Hudson about twenty miles away, and that damn pizza better be hot, and we were to take Joe's truck.

Buttser ordered the pizza and off we went. The other two were freaking out on how to keep the pizza hot—like stick it under the hood, maybe. I said, "Mellow out and don't worry."

When we got to the pizza place in Hudson, the pizza was just coming out of the oven. As they boxed it, I ordered a coke, took the box, opened it, sat down, and started eating the pizza. Joe and Bobby freaked out, yelling, "What the hell are you doing?"

I said, "Shut up and enjoy the pizza." They were too upset to eat and just sat there, so I enjoyed the pizza by myself.

Then, just as we were leaving, I called a pizza place two blocks from the clubhouse in South Saint Paul. I put the pizza box from Hudson under my arm, went out to the truck

with Joe and Bobby, and headed back. When we got to the second pizza place, our pizza was done about three minutes after we arrived. I switched boxes. We went to the clubhouse, put the box down, and Buttser tore it open and put a piece in his mouth. He burned the shit out of himself.

They couldn't believe we'd gotten the pizza back that hot and tried for days to figure it out. Finally one of the other prospects cracked. So much for brothers sticking together.

Then there was the time the frog patch came up. It was a club custom that each prospect would have to eat a live frog. (I never found out why.) But if you could think of something really gross to do with the frog first, you didn't have to eat it. The other prospects just sat there dumbfounded, but I grabbed the frog, went over to the dog the club had, lifted his tail, and stuck the frog up his ass. (The dog never came near me again.) The club members didn't realize who they were dealing with—I was always one step ahead.

I finally made patch (became a full member), and within two years I was president. I guess I was a little too radical for them, though. I liked to go out and party with the other clubs around town like the Los Valientes and BPMs, but the Spokesmen were just happy in their own little corner. After about two years, they started having secret meetings behind my back, and they came up with a list of things they wanted me to do. About eight of them showed up at my shop one afternoon and said they wanted to talk to me in private. Butch, a Los Valientes member who was working for me on work release from a drug conviction, asked if I needed any help, and I said, "There's only eight."

We all went out to this roadside rest stop in Rosemount. I was really surprised that one of the prospects I'd sponsored was with them. All I could say was, "Et tu, Bobby." It sucked—such a great line and no one had a clue what it meant. They had a bunch of demands like firing Butch, me stopping hanging around with the Valientes, and about eight other bullshit ideas. I asked them what color the sky was in their world. Their response was to tell me I was kicked out of the club and to turn in my colors. I said, "You chickenshits, I quit, you have to take my colors."

Several minutes passed and they all just stood there—literally no takes. I got on my bike and rode back to the shop. As I walked in, Butch asked if everything was okay, and I said, "Yeah, couldn't be better." I took off my colors and tossed them on the floor in front of my office. I figured if those guys were going to be a bunch of no-ball pricks and not respect or stick up for their colors, I wanted nothing to do with the lot of them. I was pissed about the time I'd wasted with them, trying to build up the club only to be stabbed in the back.

After hearing what went down, my blood brother Billy, who had been in the club, quit too. They had kept everything from him. Another club brother, Todd, who was also in the dark, quit as well.

Less than a year later, after prospecting, I made patch with the Valientes. I'd started prospecting with them mostly because Butch had been after me for years to come over. He was in club retirement, but he came out to sponsor me, and I picked Gaylord, the Indian biker who'd been with the club since it started, to be my other sponsor. I didn't want anyone saying I got it easy because I knew so many Valientes members, so I picked the two toughest guys. And then, two years after that, we shut the Spokesmen down.

It's funny how people I'd hung with at various times in

my life in different areas had all come together and ended up with the Los Valientes. Like they say, the cream always rises to the top. I had the respect of the people I already knew, and I soon earned the respect of everyone else. Somehow, though, I got the reputation of an instigator. Prospects can get their asses kicked or be fined for screwing up, and I was the highest fined prospect in the history of the club, an honor I still hold. In nine months, I paid $5,000 in fines!

CHAPTER 8

TO THE CORE

It was June of 1969 when I first met Edie. We really didn't hit it off at first because she'd seen me at parties where I was always the drunk smart ass instigating some kind of mischief. The first words I ever said to her were, "What the hell are you girls doing here?"—she came with her friends to a party I was having at Howard Johnson, and they were the only ones there who weren't couples. She gave me an earful in response, and they took off.

Afterward I thought how she was a real beauty in that girl-next-door sort of way with her brown hair and green eyes—and I was smitten. I made a point of hanging out with her brother Art, who I'd known before, so I could run into her—but she still wasn't impressed. But one night we were at another party, and she and her friend Joyce had to go home but didn't have a ride. Who volunteered? None other than the jerk.

I thought maybe I'd make some points with my car, which was an olive green '68 GTX that was U.F.B. (un-***ing-believable). I mean, it even had the eight-track stereo. I was super nice on the ride home, trying to engage her in conversation, even listening to her. I was pulling out all the stops.

Even after all that, it took about five and a half months of my best behavior to get her to go out with me, and it happened to be New Year's Eve. Before we got to the party, I figured I'd swing into White Castle downtown and profile a little. Everything was great until I spilled a rum 'n' coke on her in the parking lot. She was not impressed with my finesse, but after I let her dry out a little, she was really nice about it.

At the party, as it got close to midnight, I figured that we'd kiss at twelve, and I went to get the champagne. When I got back, here was this guy trying to make the move on her. He was all puckered up, trying to get my New Year's Eve kiss. Well, he didn't end up kissing anyone that night or for about six more nights, because I punched him right in the mouth.

I think I impressed Edie by how I came to her rescue, because we dated for three months, and then I asked her to marry me. She said she wanted to think it over, and I was devastated because I wanted a "yes" right away. But I guess at least one-half of the team should be levelheaded. And three days later she accepted.

My parents loved Edie. They couldn't believe I was going to settle down with a normal girl and not some circus performer or stripper. We got an apartment on Thompson Avenue in West Saint Paul, and Edie was a saint right from the start, the way she put up with my shit. I was so insecure I wouldn't even let her go out to the pool while I was at work—what a dick. I had a really bad temper, and combined with the insecurity, I was hell on wheels. On more than one occasion, I overreacted to men paying attention to her—at first she thought it was nice someone wanted to protect her, but it got out of hand. The one saving grace was that I was a workaholic—I wanted to get her everything she desired, and I felt she deserved the best, so I did my damndest.

My friends gave us six months because I was such a party animal, but I'd been housebroken. Edie even had me putting the seat down and wiping up the sink after shaving. When we went out, we were always together. No solo runs for me.

About that time, I turned twenty-one and got the settlement from when I had lost my eye—about $22,000. We bought our first house and furnished it. I got laid off my job, but I wasn't worried because I had money now, so what's to worry about? But after about a year, things started to get a little lean, so I found another job and met Darryl, who always had some scam going, and I was an eager student. There was the solar- and wind-powered clothes dryer I designed and sold plans for at $15—or you could buy the kit with everything needed, which consisted of a clothesline, clothespins, and tree seeds, along with instructions and a notice that it didn't work well on cloudy or rainy days. Not bad for $25. I had ads in several magazines and took in over $10,000 in four months.

Then I moved on to the return business. I picked up a copy of the codes for a local chain store and a price marking gun. I would make tags with the correct number and a better price, buy several things at one store, peel off the tags, replace them, and return everything across town. I could usually make $75 to $100 every other day. But Edie caught me doing it once, and she was steaming. She said she couldn't live like this. It still went on for a while, though, until the stores got a computer system that connected them all and kept track of returns.

Right from the beginning of our marriage, Edie and I wanted kids, so we started trying right away. Edie had had

an ovarian cyst removed right before we got married, and her doctor told her it might be hard for her to conceive, but we were determined. When we finally got the news she was pregnant, we were both ecstatic, and scared. Reality set in. We were going to have a baby we were totally responsible for. Shit, what did we know? Well, we did everything by the book, except we moved to Minnehaha and White Bear where there was a killer bakery right across the street and great pizza on the corner. Needless to say, Edie gained about forty pounds, but she still looked great, just so happy and naturally beautiful.

As the day got nearer, I got more and more scared. Man, babies are so little and fragile, and all the things that can happen! I was a nervous wreck by the time I got the call that her water had broken. I was in South Saint Paul, and I got to the hospital before she did. She wasn't quite the glowing, happy woman I had left that morning—well, she was glowing, but not with happiness. I took her hand to calm her down, and she almost broke mine letting me know that this was going to be an only child.

After a long labor, the staff wheeled her into the birthing room. I prayed for everything to be okay. Finally I got the news that I had a nine-pound, ten-ounce baby girl, which came as a real surprise because the doctor had predicted a small boy—but who cares? I thought she was the most beautiful baby ever born with her dark hair and cute little face, and when I held her, the feeling was indescribable. I was so proud I helped to make this little person, and I vowed to do everything in my power to make her happy and protect her as much as I could.

I was so excited I even went out and got new mags and tires for the car so Jessica could ride home in style. She was set with a new crib, tons of stuffed toys, and three grandparents who couldn't get enough of her. She was a great baby with a real will of her own, and she let us know if she wanted something. I would give my life for her smile.

But then after several months of normal check-ups, doctors started to show some concern. Tests revealed that Jessica had cerebral palsy. I was devastated. What did I do? Did I cause this with all the drugs I took, or was it the doctor, who I'd picked? Edie told me that Jess was so big that she hadn't gotten enough oxygen during birth and it had hurt her brain.

As Jessica grew, the CP became more apparent. Her right side was affected, and she had to go through several operations on her hand and leg to straighten them. It's just not fair how this beautiful little girl could have this happen. I would have traded with her in a minute. The surgeries were total hell—I just begged God not to let anything happen to her, and Edie was a total rock, holding things together. I know I'd have never made it through without her.

I guess I really went overboard. I went into super-overprotective mode with Jess. I couldn't let her out of my sight. I remember one Saturday night when she was about five and my mother wanted her to stay overnight to play with my little sisters. About 9 p.m. I couldn't take it anymore and I went over to pick her up, saying I forgot about a doctor's appointment she had the next day. Everyone gave me shit because there were no doctors' appointments on Sunday back then. Busted.

The overprotectiveness was so bad that Jess never had a bike when she was growing up—too dangerous. I didn't let her leave our yard until she was about nine. When she started school, she was in a special class because of the CP, so a bus picked her up—a relief for me until after we'd

moved, when I started worrying that the bus would bring her home to the wrong address. I drove to school the first day and followed her bus home, but about halfway through the route the bus driver got worried because he was being followed and called the cops. Jess looked out the window and said, "Oh, no, that's my dad!" and things got straightened out.

At about fourth grade, Jess was mainstreamed into a regular class. She was upset because several boys were picking on her, and calling the school didn't help. It was two brothers who lived near us, so I decided to act like a civil adult and went over to talk to their dad. This guy was a total jackass—he said, "Kids will be kids." Then I informed him that if his kids picked on my daughter again, I would be back, tear his head off, and kick it up his ass. If that wasn't clear enough, I'd demonstrate right now. I guess he heard that because he called them, smacked them, and gave them orders to stay away from Jessica, which they did after that.

When Jess was about six, we learned that Edie was pregnant again. We were just as happy as the first time, but not as scared. Danielle was born on a nasty winter day after an ice storm, and I fell down the back stairs of our duplex when I went out to chisel out the car. Then I helped Edie down and off we went. This time we had a different doctor and things went okay—after four hours I had another beautiful daughter.

It must have been really hard on Jessica and Danielle growing up with me as a dad. We moved nineteen times in thirteen years because I was always changing jobs or skipping out on the rent. But when I moved out because of my drug dealing, though, I talked to them almost every day and spent all the time with them I could. Edie never used the kids to try to get to me no matter how strained our relationship was. She was great.

Later, after Danielle was married, I saw that Edie and Jess were having a tough time financially and asked them if they wanted to move into the first-floor unit of the duplex I'd bought from my sister Sue. (My mother lived upstairs.) I told them I'd move into the finished basement. I guess some people thought we were getting back together, but that wasn't the case—it was just nice we could get along. I always felt bad she had me at my worst time—I was prone to violent outbursts (but I never hit her). There was this time when I slammed into a car on purpose because the driver was blocking me when I tried to back out of Snyders Drug on White Bear. I honked and honked, but he didn't move, so I thought he was just screwing with me. When he got out, he was making those hand gestures trying to tell me he was deaf, and I was so embarrassed I could have crawled under a rock. I took him out the next day and bought him another car.

I guess Edie saw something deep down in me because our marriage lasted eighteen years. She used to joke that she could have killed someone and done less time. But I was always smart enough to realize I'd never have a better wife or mother for my daughters.

CHAPTER 9

BUTCH

Picture this. He's got dark, long hair and a goatee. His shoulders and arms are massive. He isn't that tall, maybe five-foot-eight, but he's built like a tank. His eyes can see right through you. There's a little glitch in the lid of his left one. He weighs maybe 200. In high school, he made the kids call him Mr. Weyer, whether they wanted to or not. He's done hard time at Stillwater for armed robbery. People kind of step aside if he's moving in their direction.

Butch's mom was a Filipino freedom fighter, hiding up in the mountains and doing sabotage. She'd been captured by the Japanese and tortured—you could still see the rope scars on her ankles. She never forgot how to do martial arts. She married an American soldier and came to America to live. There was nothing peaceful about that house, especially with the five kids—first Maria, then Butch, then Eugene, Robert, and Tommy. After Butch's dad left, the boys were raised by his mother, who was a unique individual. Butch ended up being the toughest babysitter going. He finished high school in reform school. He had a temper that made strong men cry, even before he hit them.

I remember the first time I met Butch I was in the

Spokesmen MC and had just built a chopped Sportster. I was out riding it when I decided to stop by Butch's shop (he had one in Tanner's Lake) to check it out. After I'd hung around for an hour or so, I tried to go, but it was about 95 and humid, and my bike would start and race and then kill. After about fifteen minutes of kicking, I was pretty worn out, so I went back in the shop. Butch said he knew what was wrong, and he could fix it for $15.

Naturally I wasn't going to let him do that, so back out I went to start kicking again. After about twenty minutes, Butch sauntered out with a screwdriver and tightened up my intake manifold clamps. One kick, and it started right up. He said he was tired of watching me mess around.

It's funny—sometimes you meet someone and know this is going to be a friend or an enemy. Even though Butch knew how to fix my bike when I didn't, I had an instant kinship with him. I knew we were both alpha males, and they don't usually get along, but we were close right from the beginning. We didn't seem to have anything to prove to each other. We were just friends.

I remember before Butch retired from the Valientes and moved to Las Vegas, he stopped by the Iron Horse Motorcycle Shop where I had just started to work. He was looking over some parts we had (he'd sold his own shop) and I told him I would give them to him at cost. He looked at me surprised, and I said I owed him that for getting my bike started that time. He laughed—he hadn't forgotten either.

About a year later he came back from Vegas and stopped at my new shop, Deadeye's Custom Cycle. I had left Iron Horse and figured I needed my own shop. We started hanging around together more—he was always telling me I should be a Valiente, which deep down I knew anyway.

Then Butch got busted on a coke charge because some piece of shit snitch had set him up. He ended up in the workhouse, and I made arrangements to get him out on work release as a mechanic in my shop. I'd always thought I was a good mechanic (I told people I had a lifetime warranty on the motors I built—if one blew up, you could bring it back, and I'd take you in the back room and kill you), but after watching Butch, I felt like I should never use my tools again. He was a genius when it came to mechanics, and if he couldn't figure something out, chances were he'd dream about it at night and come up with the answer.

The longer we worked together, the better friends we became. I'd never had a friend like this before, someone I trusted right out of the gate. He was no bullshit and one of the fairest people I'd ever met, but a lot of people were really intimidated by him because he was tough. I have seen grown men piss their pants just by hearing Butch yell at them.

Butch wasn't above knocking a dickhead out if you crossed him. I remember one time when another mechanic who was working for me was running his mouth, saying that he was sick of carrying Butch and fixing his screwups. How could he think that wouldn't get back to Butch? Well, it did. The next day I came to work with a bag of McDonald's burgers and fries at about 11 a.m. Butch was already there, and he was smoking. He told me about Rock and the bullshit he was spewing, and how when Rock came in to work, I would be down to one mechanic. I hadn't seen Butch this mad before and hoped that Rock wouldn't come in to work that day so Butch could cool down.

Well, as I sat there eating my cheeseburgers (Butch was in no mood to eat), in wanders Rock. I thought, Oh shit.

Butch was behind the counter and asked Rock really calm what kind of shit he was talking. Rock just played it off with What? Who? Me? Very carefully, Butch explained the story that had gotten back to him, and Rock just stood there with this shit-eating grin.

Butch said, "I'm going to kick your ass, but you can have the first hit," and he bent over the counter with his eyes closed.

Rock knew he was in deep shit and started to mumble, "I don't want any trouble."

Butch said, "Too late," stood up, and bitch-slapped Rock so hard I think his parents felt it.

At that point, Rock was out cold on the counter, next to a truck piston I had lying there to use as an ash tray. Before I knew it, Butch grabbed the piston and peened Rock in the back of the head with it. Blood hit the ceiling and the wall, and I thought Rock was dead for sure. He slipped down the counter onto the floor like a dead snake, with a pool of blood forming around his head. Butch looked at me with a "we're in deep shit" look, and I got up to lock the door. We didn't need anyone popping in just then. I told Butch not to worry—we could put him in the basement till dark and take care of it then. (I also told him we could gut him, so when we threw him in the river, he wouldn't float.)

Then Butch left and I started dragging Rock to the basement, but halfway across the shop he came to and scared the bejesus out of me. I got him several shop rags for his head, while all the time he was whining, "Why did Butch do this to me?"

I said, "Maybe because you're a dick." (I never really liked Rock.)

Anyway, I sent him home. I'd learned why they called

him Rock with a head like that. About two hours later Butch came back, and I told him what had happened. He thought I was pulling his chain, so he called Rock's place, and when Rock answered, he just said, "Holy shit," and hung up.

Butch always teased me about that day, how I just sat there eating my cheeseburger and not missing a beat. One time I asked him if he would close his eyes and give me first shot at him, and he said, "Hell, no, because I know you'd hit me."

But even if we argued, we were like brothers. We were both pretty pigheaded, but we respected each other, and that's what made us as tight as we were. He knew I had his back, and I knew he had mine. When I prospected for the Valientes, he saved my ass on quite a few occasions, because I was always dicking around and playing jokes on the members. When I patched, I told Butch what a great prospect I'd been, and he told me the club had a hard time deciding whether to vote me in or kill me. I always hoped he was kidding.

CHAPTER 10

PHARMACY 101

I **guess** my serious drug dealing started about 1983 when I was with the Spokesmen Motorcycle Club and living in South Saint Paul. I owned a motorcycle shop on Concord Avenue almost at the Inver Grove line. It was a nice little shop with three bike lifts and lots of room for storage of parts and bikes. It was the neighborhood type—no easy chairs or waiting room, just the nuts-and-bolts real deal. A bike shop run by a biker.

Business was good, but I always needed more money. I knew some of my friends were dealing drugs and doing quite well, so I thought a little extra cash like that would be cool. I talked to several of them, and they were agreeable to getting me started. They weren't worried about me because I had a rep as a stand-up guy whose word was good.

As soon as I was ready, they showed me the ins and outs of the business regarding pot or crank (methamphetamine). I thought pot was too bulky and the money sucked, but with crank you could make some serious money, so I figured I'd sell it until I made $5,000. Don set me up with the products and taught me about cut, the process by which you can make one O.Z. (ounce) into one and a half to two O.Z.s, depending on quality. He also taught me about weighing and packaging in grams, one-halfs, quarters, or eight-balls. I decided on quarters because I could turn a $1,500 investment of good-quality shit into $2,800, less the cost of cut and Baggies.

The first O.Z. went really fast, so I picked up another one and figured I'd go two-tenths light on each quarter and make two extra quarters. Well, I made $5,000 in less than a week. It was so easy that I figured I'd go for $25,000, and then that would be enough. But I made that in less than a month, and I decided that I had found the perfect job.

All this was running out of my shop, more or less. I was putting all that storage space to use. I even had a friend to help me—as I said earlier, I'd gotten Butch out on work release. (He was doing some serious dealing too and had been busted.) He was the perfect addition to the shop because of his mechanical experience and his reputation. He'd owned his own shop in Tanner's Lake before he moved to Vegas. Then he'd come back, and now he was working for me.

One day I received a call that my alarm in the shop was going off. The last thing I needed was someone nosing around the shop, especially with the new digital scale I'd bought and the two fresh O.Z.s next to it in the basement. So I got dressed and jumped on my bike—an FLH Police Special—and headed down to the shop, only to see six cars with one-foot antennas in the parking lot. That meant the police, and I thought the jig was up. I considered taking off, but I figured, what the hell, I might as well see how bad it was.

So I pulled in and got off my bike and went inside, only to be met by the Alphabet Squad—DEA, ATF, FBI, Dakota

County sheriff, and BCA. The first thing I said was, "Do you have a search warrant?" and one was pushed in my face. As I looked to the right, there was Butch with that oh-shit look, handcuffed and shackled in chains. The shop was being torn apart, and not too nicely, I might add.

As the search went on, they kept finding guns that were placed around the shop in case of robbery. (Can't be too safe.) They found the Snake Charmer shotgun, one Mack 10, two 357 Magnums, a Smith & Wesson Model 10, and a 44 Bulldog. They'd also found my two O.Z.s of crank and a pound of pot that was so bad I couldn't have given it away—I'd forgotten all about it.

Well, when they were searching, one of the officers commented that there was just too much shit with all the used parts, and with that he tossed an air cleaner at the wall. It bounced off the tops of two fifty-gallon drums, hit the wall, and fell to the floor without opening. My heart stopped beating at that because the air cleaner had a quarter pound of coke in it. The guy looked at me and asked what was wrong. "You look terrible," he said. I told him this was all a little much.

The phone kept ringing and they kept answering it, until finally one of them said in a sarcastic voice, "You guys really do work on bikes down here." I guess he was surprised that we had real careers.

After about two hours, they decided enough was enough, so they took us to the Dakota County jail. It was funny to see the two of us—they kept Butch in shackles because they were intimidated by him, but me they walked out without even any handcuffs. When we got in the squad cars they started in on what a good guy I was and how I was just mixed up with the wrong people—just using me with all that

"good cop" shit. I figured I'd use this and see if I could get them to go through the drive-thru at the Hardee's in Hastings, since I hadn't eaten all day and was really hungry. They wouldn't do it, though, no matter how I tried.

When we got to the jail in Hastings, it was pretty hectic at the booking. As I was being printed, I heard them talking to Butch in the outer room, asking him if he had anything to say. He said, "Yes," and then after a short pause, he said, "F*** you and f*** off." (He always had a way with words.) Then when I was waiting to be mugged, I heard something hit the floor—the lens fell off the camera while they were taking Butch's mug shots. "Shit, he broke the camera!" someone yelled.

Then they took me upstairs to the cell block, but first they made me change into an orange jumpsuit that was so small I had to walk bent over so I wouldn't smash the boys. When I finally got to the cell block, I slid out of the top of the jumpsuit and tied the arms around my waist. That meant I was bare chested, and there were about ten guys looking at me. I didn't know what they were in for and didn't really care. I checked out the accommodations and decided I'd take the room with just one bunk (the others had four bunks or two bunks, and I like my privacy). "Who's in my house?" I asked, and some guy piped up, "That's *my* cell." Well, after a short discussion during which I introduced myself, he moved out and I settled in.

There were three tables with benches built into the floor in the open space outside the cells, and about 4:30 I heard the food cart coming to set out supper there. I thought, Great! But before it got to our cell block, two detectives showed up and said they were taking me to questioning. I said, "Hey, I wanted to eat first," but they weren't interested, so downstairs I went.

Once the questioning started, they hit me with the old good cop/bad cop routine and told me that if I wanted to save myself I'd better start talking because Butch was already telling them it was all mine. I said, "Yeah, sure," because I knew Butch wasn't saying anything same as he knew I wasn't saying anything. They just didn't realize some people have scruples and don't snitch or make up shit to get off. You got to stand up and be someone who can be trusted no matter what.

After about an hour, they figured they weren't going to get anywhere, so back up I went. I walked in, and dinner was all gone, so I was pissed and started looking in the cell for anything from the canteen. As it happened, I found several candy bars, and when I asked if it was okay to have them, everyone was very agreeable. After eating, I laid down on the bed—I was really drained, and off to dreamland I went.

In the morning, I awoke to the sound of the food cart and was up like a shot. When they started putting the trays on the tables, I was quite happy. But after eating what was on my tray, I noticed everyone else was still sleeping, and I thought, Hmmm. Before I knew it, I had eaten all the breakfasts—they weren't exactly three-star, but not bad. Of course, as everyone got up and came to look for breakfast, they all got quite upset. All I said was, "You snooze, you lose." I can tell you that they were all up for lunch, and we seemed to get along well as long as I was full and happy.

In the meantime, Butch had been put in the other cell block. All was going as good as could be for him—he had

the single and knew the trustee, who kept him abreast of what was going on. Butch said to say "Hi" to me, and the trustee told Butch that I'd been strong-arming my cellmates and eating all their food, besides taking the room with a single bunk. Butch laughed and said, "Yeah, that Deadeye can be a real prick sometimes."

After lunch, the guards took me over to the courthouse for my preliminary hearing, and I was brought into a small waiting room before my appearance. I ran into a friend in the holding cell who had been brought over from Oak Park Heights, and he was surprised to see me. He started talking about this murder and how they had found his glasses under the body, but I told him to shut up and said, "How about those Twins?" The last thing I needed was to be an accessory to a murder at that point.

Then I got served, and they were talking $50,000 bail. Fortunately, I got hooked up with a P.D. (public defender) and ended up with O.R., which meant I was released on my own recognizance. They actually trusted me to come back for the trial. I couldn't believe it.

When I went back to the jail and got released, I couldn't get anyone to pick me up, so I was out there hitchhiking on Highway 61 when a friend drove by and gave me a lift. I asked him to take me to the shop—I planned to get my bike and pick up the undiscovered coke from the air cleaner. When we got there, I asked him to come with me and watch the lot. I went to grab the coke, and just as I got to it, he said the cops had just pulled into the lot. I thought, Shit, they let me out to see what I would do!—so I ran into the bathroom and dumped everything out of the air cleaner and flushed and flushed as fast as I could.

Then I heard Todd say, "Hey, they were just setting up a

speed trap!" I about fell over—why me? Why me? Now I was going to owe for that, too. How was I going to explain to Butch about his coke? Well, I got my bike, said "Bye" to Todd, and went home.

The end of all this is that Butch got released on $50,000 bail. I figured I might get off altogether because my shop had two legal addresses, and the search warrant had been for only one. My public defender said that wouldn't have made any difference, but I found out later that he used to work for the prosecutor's office—not good! I had charges with a total of fifty-five years hanging, but I got off pleading guilty to just two of the seven charges—possession of pot and possession of pot with intention to distribute. (No one paid any attention to the fact that the pot was rotten to begin with.) I got sixty days in jail with work release and three years on paper (probation) with a $3,000 fine.

Before Butch's court date, I decided I would take the whole rap for everything. After all, Butch had seven years hanging from his previous coke bust, and I was clean and had less to lose. When I was called to the stand by Butch's attorney, I told the court how Butch was an innocent bystander and had no idea what I was up to. With my testimony and no real evidence, they dismissed all charges against Butch.

Later, I used to tease him that the cops had told me they'd change my name, move me anywhere, give me money if I'd testified against him. They even offered to set me up with a job, but the idea of one of their jobs didn't sound good to me. Everyone thought that was a great story.

During my three years of probation, I was court ordered to complete a rehab program for drug users. I did it (on the third try), and they looked at me as a model citizen because

I saw my parole officer, did piss tests when they were required, and didn't drink or use (at least not when I'd get caught). The real story is in the next chapter. I did join the Los Valientes Motorcycle Club, but no one bitched about that.

People couldn't figure why I took the rap for Butch, but he'd have done the same for me. We are both old-school bikers and believe that you stand up for your friends.

CHAPTER 11

NO MATTER WHERE YOU GO, THERE YOU ARE

When you're talking about rehab, one thing that gets totally lost on a lot of people is that if you don't want to change, no amount of court orders, threats, or bribes will work. I've been to rehab three times, and I know.

It seems a lot of programs work on the physical addiction but miss the real problem—why did you start? There needs to be a reason to want to escape your situation. I've never known anyone who was happy with him or herself and surroundings who said, "Hey, let's get wrecked." No, they want to stay straight and experience life, not hide from it.

The first time I was in rehab, I was court ordered to treatment after the bust at the shop and me being put on probation. I chose a center in South Saint Paul. I really felt I had no problem—I was just dealing and my customers had the problem.

The first day I showed up and met the group—an older man who drank, a woman who liked pain pills, a teen who was a pothead, and two crankheads. The woman who ran the group never drank or did drugs—what was she doing there? You can't get this knowledge out of a book. The book can't tell how your whole body shakes just thinking about that drug or drink you need, or how everything you once held sacred falls by the wayside just to fill that need so deep inside of you that everything else becomes secondary. How your mind races with the thought of just that one high, knowing it's wrong, but everything is on override, forget everything and everyone. You just want to get better, just want that high that makes everything okay even if it's just for five minutes. You just need to fill that want—it's stronger than sex, hunger, even love, it's the light at the end of the tunnel, the air in your lungs after holding your breath, it's the sun on your face after a long storm, it's life. You can't get that from any book, so how can you even think you can tell someone how or why to quit?

Not surprisingly, we did not hit it off. When she asked me what I'd like to be called, I said, "Mr. Hayes," and it was downhill from there. I went for two weeks, and every time before I went, I'd stop off at Bugg's for three or four drinks. Then I'd do a rail of coke, put on my sunglasses, and show up to listen to her shit about how the old guy in the group shouldn't drink near beer because it was a crutch. Shit, he was seventy, and if he needed his near beer to get through the day, so what? Or how the older lady who had a fear of blacks should be ashamed for judging people. Shit, she had never even met a black person until three years before, but she grew up with all the bullshit stereotypes pounded into her head. You can't expect a person to just change overnight—you have to be more understanding.

Well, when I voiced my opinion, I was kicked out, and she contacted my parole officer and told him what a poor attitude I had. But before I saw my P.O. the next week, I had my ass covered and was in a new program, keeping my mouth shut and playing the game. I almost made it through that one, only about four days short, when the old me slipped out and answered several questions truthfully. I guess I was caught up in the moment.

Needless to say, I had to kiss some ass to get into a new program. If I didn't, it was In-Patient for me, and when you're court ordered, you stay till they say so. Well, I got into the program at Mounds Park and went through with flying colors, even did my aftercare. They said what a good example I was. Yeah, if only they knew I was still abusing, but just kept my opinions to myself. (Those were the days before surprise drug testing.)

Don't misunderstand me. Treatment is great for those who want to get better, and AA is just the ticket for lots of people who find the support to stay clean, but only if it's really what you yourself want. It's funny—every time I went straight, it was because I was sick of being sick, and I was lucky it finally stuck. Otherwise I know I'd have been dead long ago.

About three months after getting off probation (they made me do the whole three years), I had gotten back into dealing, but this time I was serious. The last year I was on paper, I'd nurtured a friendship with a dealer. Even though he didn't like doing business with bikers because of our bad reputation, he was comfortable with me because he'd checked me out, and I was solid. I started small with him, just quarter pounds, but within months I was up to ten L.B.s a month on credit with a thirty-day rollover. You didn't want to be late on that payment—they didn't have compound interest, but compound fractures instead. I didn't want someone like me at my door.

After a little while, I had at least five people selling for me, and I was making a killing. I had so much money I didn't know what to do with it. I had moved out of my house because I didn't want to endanger my wife and kids. In my warped way of thinking, as long as they had money and the things they wanted, they were okay, but I didn't realize what they wanted was just a plain old dad and husband. I always thought the money would make them happier than I could because I couldn't even make myself happy.

It's freaky how you get sucked into all the bullshit and start believing it. I found out about money and power being super aphrodisiacs—boy, were they right. Everywhere you go, people want to know you and be your friend. Everywhere I went, someone wanted to please me. It got so common it lost the thrill, and things started getting kinky just to make it interesting—two girls, three girls, orgies, strange places—just to get the juice flowing again. It was the same with being able to buy what you wanted anytime you wanted it, but that got boring really fast. I always felt like something was missing—money didn't do it, sex didn't do it, drugs and booze didn't do it. What was wrong? I just spent the money as fast as it came in.

I think back now and I realize that deep down I felt guilty about what I was doing. That's why I would keep a bag in my kitchen where I put all the change, dollar bills, and fives that I got. Then once a month I'd take the whole bag's worth and buy things like mittens and warm hats for the homeless shelters in Saint Paul and drop them off outside their doors in the middle of the night. It made me feel better and kept me from thinking about how I was responsible for destroying people's lives. I always told myself that I sold good stuff and took care of my customers, and they were all adults after all, and if it wasn't me, it would be someone else.

When I got depressed, I would power shop. Not jewelry or cars or clothes—I would buy houses. At one time I had seven houses—three duplexes, two lake homes, and two regular houses. Back then you could buy a house with just $5,000 or $10,000 down on a contract for deed. First I'd bought an old brick duplex in South Saint Paul with a great view of the Mississippi. Then I lived in a cabin on Third Lake in Forest Lake for a year. It was a great one-bedroom with a fireplace and a three-season porch—and an eight-person hot tub.

For once I got involved in decorating where I was living. I went with the country look—pine tables in the living room and dining room, cloth place mats with matching napkins in pine napkin rings. It was right out of *Country Living* magazine, if there is such a magazine. I even went out and got a twenty-four-foot pontoon and a dock. Late at night, I'd go out there, lay on the dock, and watch the stars. If it was raining, I'd just sit in the rain.

After a while, Butch's brother Robert came out to show me the ins and outs of lake life with a big boat. Up till then, the only experience I'd had was paddling my gas tank when I was a kid back in East Saint Paul. When we were out the first time, he was waving to everyone and they were all waving back. He said, "Hey, Deadeye, you have to learn the lake wave because everyone here is so friendly."

I just said, "Bullshit, I don't want any new friends dropping by." I just wanted my privacy.

After about a month, I was back in party mode, chasing happiness, women, or whatever. I did buy a cute little rambler on Second Lake—it had pine paneling throughout, a big bathroom, and a great kitchen. The funny thing is that I forgot about it for over a month after I bought it. Too much partying and roaming around, I guess. But one day I was driving down Scandia Trail when I just happened to look over and say, "Hey, I own that house!" I turned around and went down there, but I had to break a window on my own property to get in because I had no idea where my key was. I guess I was looking for a home some way, but I just couldn't sort out where I was supposed to be.

CHAPTER 12

THIS OLD HOUSE

When I left the house on Fifth Avenue where I was living with Edie and the kids, I moved about seven blocks away into a brick duplex on First Avenue that I'd bought. I just fell in love with it—it was on two lots with two bedrooms down and one in the unit upstairs, with a great view of the Mississippi River and the 494 bridge. It was rundown, so I started fixing it up with a new furnace and windows. The yard needed lots of work, too—bushes overgrown, cracked sidewalks, and so on.

As it happened, I knew someone who did yard work, and he owed me money, too. I'd lent him $300 with the agreement that he'd pay me back $600 on the next Monday—I knew he was going to buy drugs from someone else, not me, so it's 100 percent interest. It turns out the other person never shows up, and he spent the $300 with me anyway—but he still owes me $600, and he knows how it works. So on Monday he comes with $550, and I say, "You still owe me $50." He says, "Okay," but he dodged me for four months, thinking I'd forget all about it.

Now I call him up and have him give me an estimate for the yard work. He shows up and says, "$500."

I say, "Great, that's just what you owe me."

He says, "It's only $50!" and I tell him he forgot about the interest. He whines for a while, but in the end he does the work, and I pay him $250.

A lot of crazy stuff went on at that place for the year and a half I lived there. Some of my customers found out where I lived and would show up at three or four in the morning, stand outside, and yell up to me on the second floor because they wanted more. They were like cats in heat. This was one of the reasons I stopped selling coke—I really didn't need some girl yelling up to me at the top of her lungs, "I'll give you a blow job if you'll let me come up and score!" Neighbors notice things like that.

I had several different tenants on the lower level, but I never called them renters because I only got three months' rent all the time I owned the place. My first tenant was Terry L. She worked at Bugg's and was going out with one of my club brothers. She lived there for six months—what a trip. There was always a party going on downstairs. I remember when she somehow got a car lot to take her car in trade, and they gave her a new Camaro before her credit check came back. Well, her and Odie, my club brother, loaded up the car and took off for Phoenix with $150 cash and a full tank of gas. That was on a Friday night, and on Monday morning I started getting calls from the car lot—they wanted the car back because no one would finance Terry, and she'd given my phone number as her landlord on her credit check. I told the salesman, "Good luck."

Well, while they were gone, the story got back to me that one of the local detectives told several people that I'd sent Terry and Odie down to pick up some crank for me. I went right to the South Saint Paul Police Department and told the detective I wouldn't send those two to the store to get milk and bread for me, let alone drugs. Not one of my smartest moments—all I did was antagonize him.

They did get back after a while, and the car lot got the car back, and she moved out. Then I got another tenant, Terry C. (It's funny about these names—I knew so many Terrys for a while, and when I broke up with my second wife, Lisa, the next eight girls I went out with were all named Lisa. It got to be a joke.) Anyway, Terry C. moved in, and her and her two kids and husband stayed for six months without paying rent, but they saved enough for a down payment on their own house. I was beginning to see a pattern developing, but, shit, money was the least of my problems.

Next, one of my club brothers, Willie, moved in with his wife and two kids. I think he was there about two weeks when he moved out and in with his girlfriend. His wife and kids were there for about five months when one day she asked me about fixing some broken windows in the basement. "Sure," I said, "once I get some rent." Here she thought Willie was paying the rent for them. Oh well.

Even with the rent hassles, I still really liked the house. I had been living there for about four months when I got this new girlfriend. (Her name was Terry, no shit.) I had met her one Sunday night when I was bartending at Bugg's. Her and her boyfriend, this guy who rode with another club, had gotten into a fight, and he left her there. Here's this well-endowed, sandy-haired blonde who looked a lot like Mariah Carey. She was a real free spirit and no one to be around when she was drinking tequila—I shudder just to think about it. (Actually, I had met her first when she was seventeen and going with this Hell's Outcast I knew.) Well, I told her I'd never leave a good-looking woman like her in a bar

all alone. Then one thing led to another, and she ended up back at the clubhouse with me. We walked in, and there was another brother, Dirty Don, who lived there upstairs. (I also kept a room upstairs for emergencies.) She asked who that was, and I jokingly said, "My dad." (Don was only about five years older than me.) Terry and I spent the next three hours working on math—I wanted to see how many times thirty-eight could go into nineteen. (Math can be fun.) After we got done cramming, she asked to borrow the phone, and she called up her boyfriend to say she was sorry for the fight and she was over at her girlfriend's house. They made up, and she asked me to drop her off by her house.

Shortly after our first get-together, me and her boyfriend were on a time share program with her. She would float back and forth. I used to call her "Boomerang" because every time I threw her out, she came back several days later.

Now the Terrys weren't the only women in the duplex. Believe it or not, the place was haunted by this little old lady who must have lived there earlier. She was a real hoot—things always went missing from downstairs, and some of Boomerang's things also. Then they'd turn up in the weirdest places, like a comb in the refrigerator or jewelry with the pots and pans. Terry C. had birds in several cages with big spring locks, and she would always come home to the birds out of their cages. The upstairs was always like a sauna, but when the old lady was around, you could see your breath. On several occasions I caught a quick glimpse of her, but she never messed with me. I think it was because I took care of the house and I cared about it like she had.

It's funny—after I sold it, I ran into a tenant and he asked me if anything strange had happened there. He told me how they couldn't keep clocks at the right time, no matter what kind they were—electric, wind-up, or battery. Weird.

Well, all good things must come to an end. I was really too hot to stay in the area, with the dealing and all, so I decided to move to a small cabin I'd bought. On moving day, several of my club brothers stopped by to help and keep an eye on my movers. Willie was helping out in the kitchen and asked me what he should do with the stuff in the refrigerator and freezer. I told him to just throw it out, but he said he'd keep the freezer stuff and started to bag it up. When he dropped a box of Jimmy Dean's Pork Sausage, out popped $2,000 in hundreds held together with my trademark red rubber bands. I hear, "Deadeye, you better come in here," and I walk in to see four boxes from the freezer with a total of $8,000 lying on the floor. I'd totally forgot all about it. I was so happy I told Willie to keep the first $2,000 he'd found, but he said, no, I'd always been there for him and he was happy to help me out.

It's funny—now that I'm straight and really have to work for my money, I think about those sausages and check the freezer, hoping.

CHAPTER 13

IF I HAVE TO EXPLAIN, YOU WOULDN'T UNDERSTAND

Bikers? I've always been of the belief that bikers are born, not made. Real bikers, that is. We must have an extra gene or chromosome or something that gives us this "I'll live like I want whether you approve or not and screw your rules of how everyone assimilates with everyone else" attitude.

To begin with, we're not challenged just by the idiots in cars who pay no attention to anybody riding by because they've got their heads so far up their asses. Bikers are always trying to prove themselves—who rides the most, who gets the most women, who kicks the most ass. It's the basic tribal lifestyle, and the biker clubs make it official.

At the top of the club food chain are the 1% clubs like Hell's Angels. People call them the 1% clubs because way back there was a rally at Hollister, California, and some of the clubs caused quite a lot of trouble. A representative of the AMRA (American Motorcycle Riders Association) said all the trouble was caused by 1 percent of the motorcycle riders, and this was embraced as a badge of honor.

My club, the Los Valientes, is considered an outlaw club

because we run a three-piece patch and claim an area. We ride with the best and are ready for any test—it's like the jungle because any sign of weakness will be smelled right out. Even your own brothers will push you just to see that they can count on you in a tough spot. There's nothing better than a good old ass kicking to get the testosterone flowing, a good old bare knuckle, knock-down, drag-out fight. No guns or knives—most of the time.

One of the best fights I had was with my brother Butch—I had screwed up and not taken care of some shit, and he was looking for me. I went right over to the shop. Gaylord was in front and said, "You're in deep shit—Butch is pissed at you."

"That's why I'm here," I said—I figured that Gaylord could mellow things out if we got out of hand. As Butch was walking through the back room, he saw me, and grabbed a bat. Gaylord was out the door in a flash, and I knew what a wildebeest feels like when the lion looks at him. We met like two head-on trains, and the aftermath wasn't pretty, but it was settled, and we were joking about it a few days later.

Each biker wears his colors, a denim or leather vest with patches. Our colors are like our Holy Grail. They tell people who we are and what we represent. Your colors are what you've worked so hard to attain, starting out with your prospect patch letting everyone know you have been chosen for the privilege of trying to become a member of the club. Prospecting is a period when you get to know each other and see if this person is really someone you can trust and really want to join the family, which is what motorcycle clubs are. Then, if you're lucky enough to make it, you receive the top rocker and center patch, which make

you a full patch member, a brother. There are other patches you can wear on your colors, too, that denote if you have done a certain thing for the club or if you've achieved certain levels.

Our colors are never to be touched by outsiders—it shows a lack of respect. On more than one occasion, I've seen respect lessons doled out to someone who just came up and started touching and asking, "Hey, what's this for?" (If you have to ask, you don't need to know.) Your colors are something that you'd never give up or allow to be taken from you. Most people would die rather than have that happen

A biker's bike is more than a mode of transportation or something cool to pick up chicks with. A biker customizes his bike with special parts until it's exactly the way he wants. A biker customizes his bike to make it his own creation—part of himself—so when you see a certain bike, you know that's so-and-so. I have known bikers to go without just to keep that bike up or get that extra something for it. It's like a second body, but on wheels.

And everyone notices the tattoos. Today, tattoos are as common as cell phones with everyone—Beavis and Butthead, lots of shit. But with us bikers a tattoo means something and has a purpose—to intimidate people, to honor someone, whatever. All of my tattoos have a story and a meaning, like the graveyard tattoo with all of my fallen brothers' tombstones. I wear their names—Stan, Mongo, Doc, Tooter, Willie, Butch, Michael—with pride. This is my way of paying tribute.

Our leathers that we wear are important, too. They have a purpose—to keep you warm if it's cold or raining, especially if you're on a run in the middle of bad weather. The leathers also keep you from getting road rash if you go down. I don't wear my leathers to walk around in like some knight, saying, "Hey, this is my suit of armor, look at me." I wear 'em for necessity.

Sometimes we don't get treated with the respect that everyone deserves. That's another thing a biker has to put up with and deal with by making clear just how things stand. I remember once when I was out riding all day. It was about 3 a.m., and I pulled into this little diner to warm up and get a little something in me. When I got there, there were only two other people in the place, a trucker and a guy who looked like he had had a rough night at the bar. I ordered my breakfast and was about halfway through it when two other guys and their dates came in. They sat in a booth right across the counter from me. The guys looked like college jocks with that "look at me I'm so cool" attitude, but the cuties with them were paying more attention to me. They kept looking and smiling and playing the flirting game, talking about my tattoos for about five or six minutes.

I could see Jan and Dean were getting pissed that their dates were paying so much attention to the scooter trash. One of them said loud enough for everyone to hear, "Tattoos are a sign of low intelligence." Well, everyone just stopped and looked at me. I sat there eating my eggs, and I thought, Why waste my time—I won't even acknowledge him. But after about three minutes, I looked up from my food, stared at him, and said in a low, controlled voice, "A real sign of low intelligence is saying that to someone who could rip off your head and kick it up your ass."

I waited to see if he wanted to respond. He just sat there like a little puppy who had been scolded for peeing on the floor. From the way the girls were snickering, I don't think he got any that night. Plus I think his balls were shriveled up like raisins.

I remember years ago me and Butch were talking that the real biker was getting to be a thing of the past, thinking that this is how the old gunslingers must have felt around the late 1800s when times were changing. It's true that the biker lifestyle is a rough one, and I'm glad both my daughters don't like bikes. They're dangerous, and this way of life is especially hard on the females. But we live this hard life by choice. We accept the dangers of the road and live life to the fullest. We believe everyone should make their own decisions and stand up for what they believe.

There's a lot of discrimination against bikers. I think it's because we choose to live the way we want and stick it in people's faces. After all, we could just fit in and not rock the boat if we wanted to live like that, but we're not good little robots. If it looks like fun, we'll do it. We know what it's like to be men.

CHAPTER 14

NOT ACCORDING TO SPOCK

Both my daughters have said that growing up with me was never boring. I've asked them on several occasions if I was a bad dad, and they both said they wished I'd been around more. Jessica and Danielle never had any second thoughts about how I felt about them, though. I always tried to give them what they wanted, but not to the point of spoiling them. They both worked and had good work ethics, because I figured they had to learn to take care of themselves since I wouldn't always be there.

Both girls are always telling people about how I used to play head games with them. For example, when Danielle was real little, she asked me why my eyebrows were so big, and I told her it was because when I was young I used to rub them. Then I started to rub hers, and she said, "No, no," so I stopped. But when she took her nap, I got Edie's eyebrow pencil and drew Groucho Marx eyebrows on Danielle. After she woke up, it took her about an hour before she noticed her new eyebrows in the mirror. She freaked out, and her mom washed them off, but she was still mad at me for the rest of the day.

As it turned out, I watched the girls all the time when

Edie was working and I was home. Once when Jess was in school and Danielle was with me, I left with her to pick up her mom at the cop shop where she worked doing data entry. I wasn't planning any tricks, but things still got exciting.

Well, at the time I was driving a '60 Chevy Impala with a bad exhaust. We were on York, and I'd just turned on Arcade heading south when this cop car behind me hits the lights and pulls me over for the loud exhaust. As he runs my DL, up pops a warrant for a parking ticket I'd failed to pay, and he comes back all pumped up about how this is his turf and I'd better not be a troublemaker and take care of the exhaust. He informs me that I am under arrest and I will need to drop off my daughter with one of the neighbors. Danielle is listening to all this like it's a TV show—she's with her daddy, so it's all just a fun adventure.

There's no way in the world I'm dropping off my daughter anywhere. I tell him I'm on my way to pick up my wife, who just happens to work at the cop shop. He looks at me like "Yeah, sure," and I say, "No shit." To which he says, "You're still under arrest!" and next thing he does is put me and Danielle in the back of the squad car. Off to jail we go, and she's having the time of her life.

Finally he gets downtown and starts to pull into the annex. Who do I see then but Edie waiting out in front for me. I tell the cop, "Wait, there she is," and he stops and honks. Edie glances over, and voilà! there's her husband and three-year-old daughter sitting in the back of the cop car. The look on her face was priceless. She walks over to the car, and the first thing out of her mouth is, "What did he do now?"

The cop says I'm under arrest for an outstanding warrant

and how I told him my wife worked at the police station, but he thought, No way. Edie just glared at me and asked for Danielle. As the two of them walked away, I said, "Love ya, honey. Get bail." I'm glad she did.

But most of my teasing was a little more private. Once when Danielle was in second grade, she was starting to show that bit of her mom she inherited. She didn't like motorcycles anymore or the Harley hat and vest I'd given her. Well, one day I was helping to get her ready for school, and the only T-shirt I could find was one that said, MY DADDY RIDES A HARLEY. Knowing she couldn't read very well yet, I told her it said, "I Like My Teacher." She was all smiles, and off to school she went. When the school day was almost over, her teacher had to mention the shirt and say it was cute. "Yes," Danielle said, "It says, 'I Like My Teacher.' "

I know she's thinking she's making points, but her teacher says, "No, honey, the shirt says 'My daddy rides a Harley.' " Danielle was really upset, and I couldn't believe it when she got home how mad she was about the shirt. She still brings it up to this day.

I'm afraid I played tricks on the girls all the time, like one Christmas Eve when they had been acting up, and I told them several times that if they didn't behave, Santa would take the presents back and not leave anything. Well, they kept at it, and after they fell asleep, I moved all the presents from under the tree down into the basement. Morning came, and when they walked in and saw nothing under the tree, they couldn't believe the presents were all gone—they just sat there for about ten minutes with their mouths open, looking at each other and at the bare floor, not saying a word. Then I sent them down to the basement, and I heard these joyous yells. I knew they'd found Santa's stash.

Then there was the time I took the girls and their mom to Target in West Saint Paul to do a little shopping and pick up prescriptions. My kids and their mom were total preppies—I mean, when people would find out I was their dad, they'd ask if they were adopted. It was like the Beauties and the Beast family. Anyway, they were waiting at the Target pharmacy for a prescription, and I was just looking around by myself. I admit I did stand out at 300 pounds with my long hair past my shoulders, a full beard, tattoos covering both arms, jeans, Harley T-shirt, looking like I'd been rode hard and put away wet.

Well, I must have made quite an impression on these two blue hairs, the way they were hugging their purses. They went and huddled over by Edie and the kids, and they pointed me out to them and to the pharmacist, saying, "I think he's going to rob the place." Edie just stood there embarrassed, but the girls said, "No way, that's our dad!" I couldn't figure out what was going on with everyone staring at me and the kids laughing and these two old ladies taking off until the kids told me. Edie just gave me that "Why didn't you stay in the car?" look.

In those days, I never realized how much my temper affected the girls. Jess still teases me about how she knew when I was about to flip because I would bite my bottom lip. They still tell people about the time when we were driving in my '65 Falcon, and the car killed when I was making a left turn onto Robert. I was partly in the eastbound lane, and anyone could see I was trying to get the car started again, when this van came out of the Signal Hills parking lot. The driver just sped up like he was going to run into us, then finally veered around us trying to be a smartass. To this day, all I remember was the van coming at us and then me walking back to our car. The girls told me that somehow I got out of our car and jumped on the side of the van as it went by and just hung there hammering on the window for about a block until he stopped, probably in shock. After I got back to our car, Edie was yelling, "You crazy son-of-a-bitch!" Jess said I looked just like the Hulk, hanging on the car and yelling.

Even my way to discipline my daughters was different. When they were younger, I'd threaten them with a spanking from a plastic spoon. They got spanked only twice, but I'd have them go get the spoon from the kitchen, and they would just sit there till I told them I'd give them one more chance. This always seemed to work except for the time Danielle, who was about five, was acting up. I sent her into the kitchen for the infamous spoon. Well, out she comes with this little elflike smile, carrying the tiny plastic spoon from the picnic basket. That was the end of the spoon.

The girls used to fight like cats and dogs, and on one day in particular they were really bad. I had enough and told them they had to sit on the couch together. Well, they each sat at opposite ends, but I said, "No, closer," until they were next to each other. I said, "Now, isn't that better?" and they both disagreed. I said, "You know, you're right. Jess, put your arm around Danielle, and Danielle, you put your arm around Jess, and hug each other until I say 'Stop.' " They sat there for half an hour with Jessica's right arm around Danielle and Danielle's left arm around Jess. They still have the pictures I took showing how cute they looked.

Edie took care of most of the school stuff because I didn't want to embarrass them (like this biker appearing at a parent-teacher conference). That all worked pretty well until Jess was in the eleventh grade in South Saint Paul. A lot of parents

knew me, but only as Deadeye, not as Jess's dad. Then I had the raid on the shop when Butch and I got busted, and there was my real name in the paper. Jess had brought some rags to her shop class just after the bust, and several of my old shop T-shirts were in them. Some of the kids were actually fighting over the T-shirts, and Dan Schmidt, one of the kids who knew me, said, "That's Jessica's dad."

Now, Jess had always been sort of a wallflower with some kids teasing her, but this time they said, "Deadeye's your dad? I've heard about him." She was a little hesitant to admit it, but when she said, "Yeah," all of a sudden she became a celebrity. She even wanted me to pick her up on my bike at school, but I never did because I always tried to keep a low profile in case someone tried to hurt me through them.

Also, Danielle had trouble getting dates sometimes when the boy found out her dad was Deadeye. She even told me a story about when she started going out with her husband-to-be. They were at a party, and several people went up to him saying, "Do you know who her dad is?" I'm glad he was interested enough in Danielle not to worry, because I ended up with a great son-in-law and two great grandkids who never heard of Deadeye. They only know Poppy.

CHAPTER 15

FINDING MECCA

With all the gambles I've taken in my life, there was one place I had to end up. My luck really changed the day Butch called me and said, "What ya doing next week?" I didn't have anything going on, so he said, "Let's go to Vegas."

I thought for about two seconds before saying "Yes!" So he showed up about 5 a.m. on a Saturday morning, and I was on my first road trip with the Man. We agreed to share the driving, but I could only drive during the day because my night vision left a little to be desired. But Butch could handle that.

The first day was pretty boring going through Iowa and Nebraska. We stayed the first night in North Platte in a nice room, but the food at Long John Silver's sucked—I don't think the fryer oil had been changed in weeks. On the next day the wind was so strong it almost blew Butch's Caddy off the highway, and even motorcycles had pulled off the road. One of them had been blown into the ditch, so we stopped to check, but everyone was okay.

The next morning, I was up before Butch and watching the local TV when he woke up. "Man, you're getting your own room the way you snore," Butch grumbled. "I thought my wife was bad!"

I knew I had quite a snoring reputation because I've been woken up in motels and hotels because of complaints down the hall. But Butch didn't push it, and we were off for another day on the road after a stop at Mack and Don's for a quick Egg McMuffin.

That was the day I saw the Rockies. As we got closer, I asked Butch what that was off in the distance, and he just said, "The mountains." Shit, they just kept getting bigger and bigger, and I was amazed. I thought, If I was a pioneer, I'd have been so intimidated that I'd have set up my tent right here. None of that mountain goat shit.

I just couldn't believe the beauty and power of the mountains. You could almost feel the vibes. It was one of the most humbling experiences I've had with the contrasts of colors, the reds, browns, and blacks. The time of history, pictures of the wagon trains and hunting parties and the old Model Ts bouncing up the roads were all running through my head.

Actually, I was really surprised how all the cars just whizzed around the curves. One little white car passed us, and we were doing between 75 and 80. It went so fast we couldn't even tell what make it was, and Butch just mumbled, "Asshole." But then, after about twenty miles, we came upon a highway patrol who had pulled the little white car over. We started to laugh, wondering what the fine would be.

After that, we stopped for gas in Vail—two long-haired, tattooed, fat greasy bikers in a new Eldorado, I knew they were thinking drug dealers or car thieves—or maybe lawyers, ha! Then when we were about fifteen miles up the road, traffic came to a standstill, and we sat there for about

Kicking one back with Dad and Gramps.

With Dad and brother Bill (*right*)—king of all I survey.

Even tied to a tree, I still managed to get my hands on a gun.

Bright-eyed and bushy-tailed at age three.

Just out of the hospital after I was shot in the eye.

My parents—Shirley and Dick Hayes.

Edie and me at our first Thanksgiving together.

Edie looked so happy at our wedding. Little did she know. . . .

My Sporty and Spokesmen colors.

My first hour as a Los Valientes prospect.

Me and Gaylord, my Los Valientes sponsor.

My sponsor, boss, brother, best friend—Butch.

My brother Bill, my running partner since we were kids.

The age of innocence—Danielle and my Sportster.

My daughter Jessica—"the real thing."

Me, Danielle, Edie, and Jessica. (photo by Jason Jorgenson)

New Mexico "Toys for Tots" run with Beaver, Butch, and Sandy.

We clean up good—Gaylord and me at my wedding to Lisa.

Butch at the Los Valientes clubhouse casino.

Butch and Sandy standing up at Bill and Debby's wedding.

Still playing with guns.

Halfway into my half-gallon at Tooter's first memorial run.

'le in front
f the Paris
Las Vegas.

)ne of my many bikes.

A meeting of the minds—Beaver, Butch, and Tooter.

Tommy Gun on a roll.

other Mick.

Dominic.

Ryan—"Look into my eyes."

"Such a deal I got for you"—Butch in back of his shop.

Outside the clubhouse before a run.

little help from my friends.

eader of the pack.

The brotherhood at Butch's grave.

(photo by Jim Kuether)

an hour. When things started to crawl along, we figured it must be a rock slide or a deer. About two miles later, we saw the fast lane blocked off with a flare. There was a wheel and miscellaneous pieces for about 500 feet, then someone's luggage torn apart. Finally, all over the road was what was left of a little white car with a tarp covering the biggest piece of it—we still couldn't tell what make it was.

Neither of us said a word for fifty or sixty miles. Finally I said, "After seeing something like that, you'd think people would at least slow down for a while." But we didn't either—once we got past the accident, it was balls to the wall again.

That night we stayed in Green River, Colorado. It was quite uneventful except that I spent about two hours sitting on the dock staring up at the stars in meditation. The next morning we stopped at the local diner for breakfast—it was like going back to the '50s with the old soda fountain set up on one side with the Coke dispenser, wooden booths like from when they built the place, and several tables in the center with that old fake marble look and the tin strip around the edge. A real Art Deco meets the McCoys. About ten people were inside, including the waitress—mostly good old boys in their bib overalls and a variety of tractor and seed company caps. There were also two young girls who didn't quite fit in with their stone-washed jeans, flannel shirts, and short hair. I think they were happy to see us walk in because it took the attention off them.

The tension was noticeable when we sat down, and the waitress was paying no attention to the new patrons. Butch looked at me and just gave me that smirk that means, "They love us here." Then one of the old boys started talking about

biker trash and how the folks here don't have much of a problem with those sorts since about five years ago when three bikers disappeared up in the hills. "I don't think anyone ever found them. Too bad," he said.

I don't think one of them was younger than sixty, but something got to both of us, and Butch said, "Shit, are you really hungry? Let's get on the road," and we left. I don't think we'd been in there for more than ten minutes, but it felt like hours. I don't get nervous easily, and Butch is a rock, but something about that diner and those old boys was like *Deliverance* in the Rockies.

After that, we went through the Painted Desert—I didn't think sand, brush, and rocks could be so interesting. Butch was getting a kick out of the way I was taking pictures and getting refrigerator magnets for me and my mom at every rest stop. Then on that night we hit the Pepper Mill in Mesquite—it was the first casino I'd been to, and I was blown away with all the lights, colors, people, and gambling. I went right to the slot machines, and before I knew it, I was about $500 down. Butch told me not to lose all my money before Vegas, so I watched him for a while. He owned the table, and pretty soon, everyone was calling to him. He won about five grand starting with $125 in bets. There was so much energy that you'd think the table could almost levitate. I think I crashed around 3 a.m., and about one hour later, with my first casino experience under my belt, I was ready for Vegas.

When we got there, we pulled into the Stardust on the strip, where Butch wanted to stay, and got valet parking. Butch taught me right away that you don't screw around with parking your own car when you can have it taken care of for one dollar. We walked in and there was a craps table only fifteen feet from the front door, slots to the left, slots to the right—man, I was in heaven. After we checked in, we were told to go up front so the bellman could take us to our room. A guy with a golf cart loaded up our luggage and said, "Hop on," and off we went around the back about half a mile from the casino back door. The room was quite a letdown—only ten by ten with putrid blue paint, orange lampshades and bedspreads, and green shag carpet. Butch said, "This ain't happening! Call the front desk and get us a real room." I called, and the golf cart showed up, took us to the front desk, and then to a nice poolside room. I don't know what Butch said or did, but what a change.

I was like a little kid—I didn't know what to do because I didn't want to miss anything. After all, we only had a week. I walked around, then found Butch in the craps pit—he'd gotten our room comped. I ended up at the buffet for free because that was comped, too. I settled in for some serious slot play, but after six hours, I was a zombie, so I crashed.

The next day after I got up I called room service—man, this was living. I ate, went out to the pool, and slept for the next six days, along with the gambling. When the day came that we were leaving, Butch told me our rooms and all of our room service had been comped, so we didn't have to pay a thing. I was down about $7,000, but I still had a great time.

Then Butch said, "Let's each take $100 and hit the table one more time." It was early, around 1 p.m., and there were only four other people there. As luck would have it I got the dice and I kept them. I was on fire, the kind of roll people dream of. I was working the numbers—everyone was making money, and the pit bosses were doing everything they could to break the rhythm of the game. I mean, they

counted the chips twice, and the stick man even pushed back a seven to me after I'd made my point, which is a real no-no. They were hoping I'd throw the dice and maybe get one off the table so they could change them. I mean, I controlled the dice for forty-five minutes—I was so pumped up I was high. The table filled up once they heard there was a shooter on the table—every throw was followed by cheering and everyone was making money.

Well, I finally sevened out and I got a round of applause. I was walking on air. I really freaked when I counted my chips and I had made $32,000 including the bets Butch was making for me. He had a little over $50,000. Man, the hook was set—we floated home. I hardly remember the ride because all we could think of was that roll and the beginning of our Vegas adventures.

CHAPTER 16

THE GOOD LIFE

Butch and I took lots of trips to Vegas together, but some of them stood out. One time we traveled there for the second Holyfield/Tyson fight (Butch had us comped at the Tropicana, as well as third-row fight seats), and we took New York John (who was actually from Philly) along. He was a bigger scammer than I was, and he told me he planned to fake falling in the bathroom to get some money out of the casino. I told him this wasn't Kmart he was dealing with, but he said he had it all worked out, so I just let it drop.

When we got settled in Vegas, I went over to Butch's suite and informed him about the plan. Well, he hit the ceiling and called John in. He informed John that if he tried it, if the casino security didn't bury him in the desert, he would, and that was enough said.

While Butch was gambling, John and I hung out together, and I took him out to Hoover Dam (about the fiftieth time for me) and all the other sights. I took him to several bars, and we ended up back at the room with two young ladies—a nice redhead and a chunky blonde. As the night was winding down, we all got companionable, and I showed the redhead my part of the suite. After several hours, we came back to the living room, and there was John and Rita, the blonde, and she was giving him a hard time—something about two minutes, and she was wondering if he had just got out of prison.

Finally all three left, and I crashed for several hours. Butch called and woke me up asking why all the soaps and towels were missing from his room. Well, John had taken all the little free toiletries from Butch's room and ours, along with all the towels, and had packed them away along with fifteen or twenty towels from the pool. I couldn't believe it. He brought the towels and toiletries back to Butch, but then he found the mother lode right outside our door in the hall—the maid's cart. He must have had fifty small soaps, shampoos, hand lotions, and the rest—on the return trip he had to get another bag just for all the stuff. He was a hoot.

Neither of us was having any luck at the tables, but Butch was about five grand ahead and was on a roll. He gave us the tickets for the fight because he didn't want to go. I went to the Comedy Club at the Riviera instead, so John ended up with all three tickets. I found out later he scalped them at $400. Leave it to John.

Sunday afternoon we were hanging out with Butch. We hit several casinos, and while at the Luxor we decided to each give Butch $100 to see if he could run it up for us. Well, he put in our $100 plus his own, which was gone in fifteen minutes. Then he got out more of his own money and turned $1,000 into $7,000. On our way out he gave us each back our $100, saying he felt bad but, shit, that's the way it goes—plus we had the room, free food, and a car.

After we packed up, we went down to the craps table

with Butch, and in forty-five minutes he made $37,000. It was great. I used to get more excited than he did. I was never one to get jealous over a friend's good luck. Shit, I was happy for him.

On one of our last trips to Vegas, Butch, Sandy, and I drove out for New Year's Eve. We left December 26. It was a great drive—the weather was beautiful, no snow, and the mountains were spectacular. We stopped in Mesquite and rolled into Vegas already ahead. I had an adjoining suite next to Butch and Sandy, and the first couple days I made myself scarce. After all, I didn't want to intrude. But I did get ahold of them in time to see what the plans were for New Year's Eve. Butch told me what time the dinner was—he always had tickets to the big parties held for all the V.I.P.s. As we were bullshitting, he told me Sandy had said, "I think Deadeye had a girl in the room last night." Butch had said, "Yeah, it's an old girlfriend," and Sandy said, "Why isn't he bringing her to the party?" Butch tells her that I don't bring her around because she's a call girl, and Sandy says, "So what?" and Butch said I was sensitive because she's only got one arm, and Sandy says, "So what?—that's okay." Butch was always mind gaming with everyone, even Sandy. You couldn't tell when he was serious. Sandy believed that story for years.

Truth is, the girl had both arms, and we'd met several years before when I was living in Vegas for the winters. She was at the bar in the Trop with a girlfriend, and I was the only guy in the bar who wasn't hitting on her. She thought, What's wrong with him? and came over and started talking to me. We just hit it off and ended up going out, and I lived with her for four months before coming back to Saint Paul.

She couldn't believe how I accepted what she did and never gave her a hard time. We had a talk about it on our second date. When she told me what she did, I asked her if it bothered her, and she said, no, she had clients who were big rollers, and when they came to town they wanted to hang around with a beautiful woman, and that was about it—it wasn't really about sex. There was some sex, but only if she wanted to. Well, I really liked her, and she was a lot of fun, and I'm the last person to judge anyone, so as long as it was okay with her and she felt safe, cool.

Well, back to the party. We showed up at 9 p.m., and everyone was dressed to the nines. Even I had on a suit. The place was all set up—they had these centerpieces that were custom made, really neat looking—and before the night was over, they were all gone. I mean, people grabbed them, and it was funny at checkout to see those centerpieces packed in with everyone's luggage.

Butch did okay that trip—I think he broke even—and I only lost $2,000, which was small change compared to the party, room, food, and the New Year's Day brunch, which was not to be believed. When you walked in, there were two four-foot ice sculptures filled with jumbo shrimp, crab legs, oysters, then a table set up with salads of all sorts and tons of fresh fruit. Then there were big chafing dishes with salmon, ribs, roast beef, several different kinds of chicken, hash browns, mashed, scalloped, au gratin potatoes, hot veggies, an omelet station, open bar, and three tables set with desserts. Everyone wanted to wait on you—man, that was living!

The drive home was quite different—we hit a blizzard in Green River, and it got worse the higher we went. I mean, it was the worst I'd ever been in. We just made it through Vail before they shut the highway down—they had seventeen inches of snow. Butch said it had to get better once we got to Denver, but it actually got worse. I can't believe they didn't close the highway earlier—we kept passing all these cars in the ditch. When we got to North Platte and it finally cleared up, we got rooms in a little motel that looked like a palace to me.

CHAPTER 17

TRICK OR TREAT

I **guess** one of the most memorable casino trips was when Butch and I went to Atlantic City on a junket for Halloween. Butch was a gold card and pretty much got whatever he wanted—the casinos always made sure he had the deluxe high roller suite, and he always got me a nice suite, too. The funny thing was the staff always got the suites mixed up and would set up the bar and the food trays in my room. After checking in, I'd get a call from Butch asking if I had the food and the drinks, which I always did.

This time was no different. There were about twenty-five people in our party, and as usual Butch was the high roller. The casino (nameless because of the nature of this story) had several limos pick us up at the airport. Butch started out kicking ass at the craps table, and I had one of his gold cards so I could eat anywhere I wanted or see the shows.

First, though, I started playing Let It Ride, and after several hours Butch joined me. This game is an offshoot of poker where the object is to make the best poker hand with your three cards and the dealer's two. Shortly after Butch joined, I was dealt a king, queen, and jack of hearts, and I'm thinking I could get another heart for a flush or pair one of the face cards. Mind you, I've only got a $30 bet out there. Well, the dealer turns over a nine of hearts. I'm still just thinking a flush, and, voilà! the next card is a ten of hearts for a straight flush. This brings me six grand—I'm in shock. After forty-five minutes, the casino finally paid me—they had to check all the cards in the deck and review the video. (Everything is filmed throughout the casino.)

After I got paid, Butch says, "Now you can really start betting."

"No way, I'm going to go eat and just enjoy the moment," I said. So off I went to the coffee shop. After one of the best chicken dinners I've ever had, I decided to take a short stroll on the boardwalk, and I ran into two girls—one a knockout blonde, about five-foot-nine with short hair and a nice rack, and dressed a little slutty. The other was a beautiful Oriental girl. They start talking to me about my trip and if I'm having any luck, to which I say, "I just got here, no luck." No way was I going to mention the six thousand in my pocket.

The blonde says that I can get lucky with them for $1,000.

I cough and say, "Shit, I don't want to buy you and take you home, I only want to rent about eight inches of you for an hour!"

She talks to her friend and she comes back with a deal for $500. I'm just standing there looking at them both real hard, and she says, "Why are you staring at us?"

I shoot back jokingly, "I'm memorizing you two so I can go back to my room and fantasize about you while waxing the dolphin."

She gives me a disgusted look and says, "You cheap prick," and they stomp away.

So I retired, and the next morning I hit room service and

then the craps table. I took out $500 and stood next to Butch—as luck would have it, he just got the dice. After about fifteen minutes, I was $1,800 ahead and cashed in. Butch said, "Shit, you can't quit now that you're hot."

I said, "Yeah, it really feels different—we still have two more days, and I'm going to pace myself."

That day I walked the whole boardwalk and took a cab to the local Harley dealer to get a few T-shirts. Shit, they were $30 each, and the cab ride was $65 (which I found out later should have been about $25). Then I hit the steak house and had a porterhouse and the shrimp cocktail and several Courvoisier XOs. The bill came to $140 with dessert, so out came the gold card, and I left a $50 tip. Man, what a way to live.

I decided to hit the boardwalk for a while. It was a beautiful night with all the people dressed up for Halloween. (I went with the biker-on-vacation look.) After about an hour, I had enough and headed to my room. I couldn't have been there for ten minutes when there was a knock on the door, and I opened it to this unbelievable girl in a pirate outfit. I mean, she had a sash from her shoulder to her hip, with a sword, puffy shirt, a short black skirt with bare legs and black boots halfway up her thighs, long blond hair and dark green eyes with full pouty lips. I mean, this woman was *Playboy* material. She said, "Trick or treat?"

All I could get out was, "Yeah."

She said, "Well, can I come in, Butch?"

And I got out "Yeah" again. I offered her a drink, and my mind finally started to work. As we talked, it hit me she thought this was Butch's suite. My mind was going a thousand miles a minute thinking what to do, and I came to the conclusion that Butch was probably on a hot streak. He didn't like to be interrupted, and he was married, too, so I decided just to play along.

After three of the most memorable hours, we had come to know each other quite well, needless to say. After she left, I just sat there trying to come to grips with what had happened—mini-bar and fruit baskets are great, but man!!!

The next morning I awoke to Butch on the phone to see if I wanted to join him for breakfast, and I said, "Sure." We made plans to meet at eleven o'clock at the coffee shop. Then I was looking around my room, and sure enough, there were some remnants of last night. Shit, it wasn't just some great dream—but how do I mention this to Butch?

Well, there I was at the coffee shop with Butch, him telling me what a great night he had—he'd been $7,000 in the hole and finished $800 ahead. He hit a royal on a poker machine and had some luck playing craps. Man, he was unreal on poker machines—he must have had thirty-five royal flushes on $1 to $5 machines. I mean, I play like a fiend, but I've only had three royal flushes in all the time I've played.

We were finishing breakfast when one of the casino hosts showed up and started asking Butch how last night was, and I think, Shit, here it comes.

Butch says, "Up and down, up and down, the same old shit."

I was wishing I hadn't eaten so much because I was feeling sick, when out it came from the host—"You liked the treat I sent you? I thought you'd like her."

Butch got this puzzled look for about half a second, then turned toward me and said, "You f***ker."

All I could do was smile and say, "Yah, sure, you betcha,"

and he just broke up. I said right away, "I know you don't like to be disturbed when you're gambling, and you're married."

He just laughed, shook his head, and let out a "Yeahhhhh."

CHAPTER 18

NOWHERE TO HIDE

Some people might think it was weird, when I was making so much money dealing drugs, that I would want to get into collecting money owed to other people. This could be a dangerous line of work—maybe that's why I liked it. The juice was up, and every situation was different. It was sort of like acting in a new play every time I went out.

It all started when some friends had money owed them, and I offered to go collect it. I was a bouncer at Bugg's Bar in South Saint Paul at the time. I had lots of connections there—a good place to sell drugs, even if three undercover cops were in the room at the same time. Taping a sealed coin baggie with a quarter gram inside to the back side of a dollar bill over the eye in the pyramid and then passing it on when someone "wanted to borrow a buck" was my usual way of dealing. No cop ever figured that out.

Anyway, Buggs had a black box where he kept his bar tabs. The bad tabs from people who owed were in the back. One night when I'd been up for about three days, I took the bad tabs and went out to search for the deadbeats. I drove up and down Concord for a couple hours, hitting all the bars, but I couldn't find a one. The next day, though, they were all beating at Buggs' door to pay up. My reputation was pretty strong already, and the word was out.

When I was into collecting, I usually got assigned the ones no one else would take—a lot of gang bangers and drug addicts. I was the last resort. I got 50 percent of what I collected. Being a collector in that world is pretty dangerous business, but I was flying so high on coke that I pretty much thought I was bulletproof, and I used to get off on the juice. It made me feel alive when nothing else did.

I remember a few of the collections especially because of some of the shit that went on with them. For instance, I went to the house of a guy I'll call John who owed $5,000. When he opened the door, I saw that his wife and kids were in the front room. So I politely said I was here in regard to his debt, because I would never do anything in front of someone's wife and kids. But he immediately took my politeness for weakness and said he didn't have the money. I was really pissed about the way he acted, that little prick. He thought he was some tough guy, the little docker golf shirt wearing dickhead.

Well, I learned where he hung out to drink, so I went there and parked next to his car and waited about an hour. Then he came out with his alcohol muscles all pumped up. When he saw me, he growled, "What the hell do you want?" He figured he'd already dealt with me. Well, my head exploded, but I kept calm and polite, said he owed the money and he was going to pay. He just snickered and laughed as he walked up to me, not knowing he was about to enter the world of hurt and pain. He was so big on himself—maybe he was a big deal around the golf course or tennis court, but now he was in my world, a dark parking lot, and I was going to explain how bad he had underestimated the situation.

When he got right up in my face, I grabbed him by the balls and twisted—the look on his face was priceless. As he fell to his knees and started to whimper, I showed him just what a psychotic prick I could be and explained to him after I finished that I would be seeing him as soon as he recovered. Also, I told him that the presence of the police upsets me, so no cops.

Four days later, I called him and stopped by to pick up the money. I told him the whole thing could have been avoided if he had been civil and paid his debt.

Well, about three months later I got a call about a collection, and lo and behold it was this guy again, only now it was $6,000 he owed to another person. Off I went, and this time he was much nicer and said he would have it all later that night. I informed him that if this was a trick or setup, there were people who would deal with him on my behalf. He said he didn't want any trouble this time, and I said okay.

Like we'd planned, I showed up at 7 p.m., and he was really nervous as he let me in and invited me into the kitchen. As I followed him, I was a little leery, but the juice was flowing, so what the heck. He asked me to sit down at the table, and he sat across from me. No one else was around, and he started to explain that he had had the $6,000, but somehow his wife had come across it and took it. I was quite disappointed, as you might guess, but I actually believed him because he knew what the outcome would be if he tried to play me.

Before I could say anything to him, out comes his wife carrying this little dog, something like a Pomeranian. She just

plopped her fat ass down at the table, and he started begging her to give the money back. I'm thinking, What is this shit? Is it their version of home theater? But he seemed really sincere, and she was a total bitch, just sitting there in her marble and stainless steel kitchen and stroking that damn dog. She had no feelings for her husband—she must have known what happened before, and I swear she wanted him to go through it again. I sat there dumbfounded—she had more feelings for that dog than for her husband, as she was telling him tough shit, she'd spent the money already.

Well, as I thought about it, I figured she'd only had the money for about two hours, so I asked her husband if she'd left the house that day. He was so upset he'd never even thought about that, but he realized she hadn't and told me no. Then she snarled out that she was keeping it, and that's it. "What are you going to do, beat a woman?" she asked.

Even in my job, I never hit a woman, but I was seriously considering it now. This bitch was cold, but I don't like to swear in front of women, much less hit them, so smacking her was out of the question. All this time her husband was mumbling about getting more time, which I had been going to agree to anyway before the bitch showed up. I just sat there in disbelief.

Then, as I was looking around the kitchen trying to figure things out, I noticed a microwave. Before I knew it, I ripped the dog out of her lap, and into the microwave it went. I was wondering if I could really turn it on, but after that little shit bit and scratched me, I was right on the verge of "no problem." He knew something was up and didn't want any part of that microwave. His little face was all contorted looking out that window like a furry roast that had come to life.

Holy shit, that lady came unglued, and started to yell and cry until I thought she was having a fit. She took off to the bedroom like a nut. I looked at her husband and said, "Do you have a gun?" because I didn't know what to expect, but he said no. Then I thought of a golf club or a baseball bat. What the hell was she up to?

I was really glad when she came out with a stack of bills—$6,000 to be exact. I felt relieved because I didn't think I could have really hurt the dog—it was just a spur of the moment thing. I just looked at him and said, "I would rethink your relationship—she cares more for the dog than for you."

That was the last time our paths crossed, but I did hear that he divorced her not too long after.

The second incident was a $10,000 collection on this wannabe gang banger. I had been up for about five days when I heard that he was at this party up by Selby, so I grabbed a Mack 10, stuck it under my long black coat, and off I went. When I got to the party, I was met with some strange looks—I guess I didn't quite fit in. I asked for Bug (that was his name), and when they said he was downstairs, I went on down. There he was sitting on the couch with about six or eight other people around him smoking crack and listening to rap. I walked over to him and said, "I'm here about the $10,000." He tried to give me this hard look and lifted the front of his shirt to show me the Glock 9 stuck in his pants. Well, I pulled the Mack out, and I think he pissed himself. Everybody else just stopped like we were playing statues. I told him to put the gun and his hands on the table and everybody to sit by him, which they all did. I explained to him that I was in no mood for his little tough-guy act, and I wanted the $10,000. He choked out that he didn't have it right now.

Someone said, "What you gonna do, shoot him with all these witnesses?"

All I said was, "If I shoot him, I might as well shoot everyone else—after all, one or two or eight, it's still the same."

Well, with that statement, things changed, and everyone became quite insistent on him paying. After several calls, $4,500 was delivered to the house. I took three guns from the people there, as well as his Caddy, as collateral. He said he'd have the rest in a week.

As it happened, he showed up in four days, and I didn't recognize him because he was dressed like Joe Normal—no baseball hat, no jersey or bling, or pants hanging down to his knees. I guess he didn't like the reality of his lifestyle—it might be okay in the burbs, but in the city it was the real shit, and you could get hurt.

When I think back about it now, it seemed like I handled it the right way at the time. I really didn't spend much time analyzing things then. I hope I wouldn't have shot everyone, but with the coke in me and the lack of sleep, I couldn't say.

Those were the two times that stuck in my mind. The rest were pretty mundane.

CHAPTER 19

THE ENTERTAINMENT BUSINESS

Well, I suppose I should touch on my short-life career as a pimp. Actually it was more or less an accident.

What happened was that I had a friend who was getting married, and I got stuck with the entertainment for the bachelor party. I had a customer who worked at a strip club, and when I got ahold of him, he introduced me to a pimp he knew. In my business, you had to be a good judge of people, and as soon as I met this character, my skin crawled. I didn't like him from the get-go. He was about six-foot-three, 260 pounds, bald, and black as coal.

Now, I am not one to judge anyone because I've always lived my life not to judge lest you be judged. You never knew how people got to be who they were (or even what they were really like), but I found out you go with your gut feelings and they're usually 99.9 percent right on the nuts. So as we talked, I could tell by his body language and his not looking me in the eye that he was a lying piece of shit. I also knew he was intimidated by me, but I wasn't looking for a new friend, so what the hell.

In the end, he introduced me to one of his girls, and we talked and came to an agreement. I set up a time and place to pick her up. She was quite attractive and seemed nice—about twenty-four, maybe five-foot-nine with short black hair, 120 pounds, dressed like the girl next door. She called herself Brandy. (I knew it wasn't her real name because everyone had a nom de plume in our lifestyle.)

When the night came, I picked her up and took her to a coffee shop so we could get acquainted and she would feel more relaxed. As we talked, I asked her what her story was and how she got into this line of employment. (I can't imagine that too many girls as they are growing up pick this as a career move.) She told me her boyfriend had owed money to a friend of the pimp she worked for, and she was paying off the debt. I asked her how much and how long, and she said it was $2,500 and that she had been working for this guy for almost a year. She had to give all the money to him, even tips, and if she held out, he beat her up.

When I heard this, I was really pissed. I'd always hated bullies, and this guy was the worst kind. I asked her if she really wanted to do this, and she said it was no big deal. I felt kind of sick because she seemed so beat down about it. She said she'd been tricking for two years, and she really didn't mind the work as long as people were nice.

After that, we went off to the party. Everything went well, but it ran about an hour and a half longer than I'd expected. So when I went to drop her off, her pimp was upset and started to yell at her for not calling and letting him know what was going on. I tried to interrupt, but he said, "It's none of your business! The bitch knows the routine."

I sat there for about ten minutes listening to this shit. When he finally settled down, I asked him if he wanted a little blow. He perked right up and said, "Sure."

I said, "Let's go out to my truck—leave Brandy here."

He said, "Great, more for me," so out to the truck we went.

Naturally he headed to the passenger side, but as I opened my door, I told him that his door didn't work and he should come around to my side. As he walked around, I pulled out the bat I always kept behind the seat—a No. 8 Louisville wood, my favorite. He got his blow, all right, but it wasn't quite the blow he was expecting.

After I finished—I think I broke both his legs and an arm besides knocking him out—I pulled out the smelling salts I always carried because I didn't want him to miss the point I was making by sleeping through it. When he came to, I informed him that Brandy was coming with me, and if there was a problem, he should just let me know because I didn't have problems, I solved them. Then I called 911 to tell them there was someone in the parking lot who looked like he'd been hit by a car, and hung up.

When I went back and informed Brandy that she was a free spirit and could do whatever she wanted, she just freaked out. "What am I going to do?" she cried. "Now I have no place to live and no one to take care of me. I'll be back on the street!"

At that time, I owned five houses of one sort or another, three of which were empty. I told her to settle down and that she could stay in one of them. At that, she tried to give me some of the money she'd earned that night, but I said, "You keep it to get some of the things you need." Then we went over to get her things. I wasn't worried about him showing up because I figured he'd be in good hands soon. I just hoped he wasn't allergic to plaster.

I got her settled in one of my houses, which happened to

be semi-furnished, so she had a good start. Right away she figured I was doing this for sex—why wouldn't she? But money and sex were the least of my worries, so I said, "Thanks but no thanks—this is just a karma thing."

After about four days, she asked me if I could get her any work. I figured she was going to trick anyway, so I took care of her and found her work, which wasn't hard to do with all the people I knew. After about a month, a friend of hers showed up and asked if I could take care of her, too. She was a skinny black girl, about nineteen, with a big black eye and a fat lip. I said it was okay for her to stay, but no tricks or johns in the house, and no drugs. She agreed, and so the whole thing started.

Within four months, I had four girls living in the house. They all looked pretty good, and they were making good money, giving me half and living like they wanted. What they didn't know was that I was putting aside the money they gave me. The money I had from dealing drugs was more than enough.

It's funny—after about seven months, Brandy and I were talking, and she said she wanted to go back to see her family in Iowa. She had been talking with them and really wanted to go straight. I said, "Cool." She told me she had $1,500 saved to take with her. Then I told her I had $4,700 put aside for her, but she shouldn't tell anyone because it was a going-away present.

With that, Brandy started to cry. I think I did, too. After about four days, she said her good-byes and got on the Gray Dog and headed home. But before she left, she asked me why I never got with her, and all I could say was that we were friends and I didn't f*** my friends—that's why we stayed friends. I got calls from her for a little over a year. She was doing great—got a job, met a nice guy, all that. The last time I heard, she was still doing fine.

Other girls came and went. Most moved on, but several I helped get out of the life and get clean, so maybe I did some good somehow. I do know that the time they spent working for me was a lot better than where they'd come from.

About one year after I got out of the entertainment business, me and some of the brothers were sitting around the clubhouse watching TV. A program came on about prostitutes who had gotten out of the business, so we were all watching to see what they looked like. Then the announcer said two of them were from Minnesota, and I froze. One of the guys said, "That's Christine and Deb!" (who were two girls from my house).

We were all glued to the set. When the girls talked about the men they'd worked for, they said the pimps had all been pretty rough on them—"except for the biker," Christine said. All I could do was keep saying, "No names, no names!" I really didn't want to hear "Deadeye" on national TV, no matter how much of a compliment it was. I wasn't into being proud and bragging about that part of my life. But we got through the whole show with no names. I think I aged about five years anyway.

CHAPTER 20

BAD DAY

It's funny how many times you hear someone say, "I'm having a really bad day" because the bus is late or they spilt their double latte mocha. But let me tell you what a bad day is really like.

It was a Saturday, and I had a bachelor party to go to, and I was in charge of the entertainment and party favors as well. It was about 6 p.m. when I jumped on my FLH and set off to make several deliveries. I had two O.Z.s in eight-balls of crank in my right boot and four eight-balls of coke for the party in my left boot and in my pocket.

As soon as I left my house, it started to rain. I came down First Avenue and took a left on Southview, then a right on Third. As I passed the police station, I noticed I was going a little fast, so as I started to go down the hill, I tapped my brake. I had these shitty Goodyear tires that were as hard as wood—they broke loose, and I lost control. I crossed the oncoming traffic, slammed into a cement median, and was launched about eighty feet, only to land on the sidewalk.

I jumped up and noticed a shooting pain in my right shoulder, but no big deal. Well, here comes a squad down the hill, and it stops to see if I'm okay, to which I answer,

"Yeah, but could you help me lift the bike?—I sprained my right wrist." So we get the bike upright, and he takes off. Here I am, not even a block from the South Saint Paul Police Department. Man, if I'd been knocked out and taken to the hospital! Off come the boots, loaded with drugs, and out come the eight-balls in my pocket. The cops would have been ecstatic—all this time trying to get me, and here I'd be served up on a silver gurney!

Now I realize I can't lift my right arm, so I lift my right hand up to the throttle with my left hand and drive the bike four blocks to Edie's house where my truck is parked. (I was keeping my bike in her garage, too.) The rain gets worse, and I climb into the pickup—a '75 Ford half-ton crew cab and a real piece of shit that always overheated.

Well, I made my deliveries and picked up Bambi (the entertainment), and off to the party we went. She's upstairs taking care of business, and I'm in the living room downstairs saying how my shoulder hurts and I think it's dislocated, when Ben says, "Do you know how much pain you'd be in if it was?"

I shoot back, "Yes!" and lift up my shirt to show them that instead of my arm coming down from the right shoulder, it's just above my right tit. They freak out, and two guys take me to the ER. After several hours, I'm seen, and the doctor says my right shoulder is dislocated—like I didn't know. Well, after several minutes of manipulation and excruciating pain, everything looks normal again. The doctor puts on this sling to immobilize the arm, tells me it'll take two weeks to get better, and back to the party I go.

It's about 3 a.m., and Bambi is not in the best of moods. She would bitch if there was no work or if there was too much work—you could never keep her happy. To top it off,

somebody had her up on the dining room table, which ended up breaking and costing me $400.

Well, I say my good-byes, and I leave to take Bambi home, and she's bitching all the way about how she thought I was going to spend part of the night with her and yada yada yada. Then the truck starts to overheat, so I head for this gas station just off 94 and Snelling that I know is open all night. I pull in with steam pouring out from under the hood, the engine knocking, and the radiator making this thunking sound. My shoulder is killing me, and Bambi is bitching and whining. When I park the truck, I just happen to see two guys there that I know. I call them over and ask them to do me a favor and give Bambi a ride home. Then she starts in with what an asshole I am and how I'm pushing her off on these two guys who she doesn't even know. "I know 'em," I say, and I make it clear to them it was just a ride home for her, nothing else.

At that point, I get the water pail and go to the faucet in the men's room. As I fill the pail up, I hear this huge crash. What the hell? I open the door—no truck. I step out, and there's my truck on the island with a pump knocked over lying twenty feet away, and gas coming out like a geyser from where the pump used to stand. I just wanted to cry.

Instead, the next thing I do is walk over to the truck and start it up, thinking if it blows up, hey, it's all over. But it starts up and doesn't blow, and by that time the attendant had hit the emergency stop for the pump. I'm already pulling off the island where the pump had been, causing this awful scraping sound. The attendant comes running out, yelling, "You better not leave!" Yeah, I've got on my Los Valientes colors, the truck's in my name, and I have this baby blue sling on my arm, plus I'm drenched in gas. I'll just blend in anywhere.

Well, I figured the cops would be showing up shortly, and I had an O.Z. of coke, my private stash, so I'd better hide it. I notice the tire without a rim in the back of my truck, so I just toss the coke inside. Then the gendarmes show up, papers are filled out, statements are taken, and I tell the owner of the station, who's just showed up too, not to worry—I'll pay for the pump myself and not report it to my insurance. He says, "It's going to cost $3,500." Man, will the night never end?

So I fill up my radiator and take off. It's now 6:15, and the sun is up. It's hot and sticky and getting worse. I'm starting to itch from the dried gas, and I really need a bump, so I pull off on the shoulder of 94 and reach into the tire. I grab the top of what used to be a baggie with an O.Z. of killer coke—I'd failed to realize that there was gas in the tire from the accident. That's $1,800 gone.

I'm really feeling like that little guy in "Li'l Abner" with the cloud over his head as I head to Edie's to maybe get a little sympathy, but the truck starts to overheat again. I figure I'm only about a half mile from her house, so I'll make it—yeah, like that's going to happen. I start to turn into her alley, and the truck dies half out in the street. I try to start it, but no luck, so I just leave it there and walk to her place. I knock on the door, and she yells, "Get your ass off my porch!" I'm reeking with the smell of gas, my right shoulder hurts like hell, it's hot and muggy, I haven't slept for about two days, I'm in the hole to about $5,500, and I have to walk seven more blocks to get home.

I'm later notified my truck was in Impound, where I hope

it rotted. I went to pay for the gas pump and saw that it was back on the island, dents and broken glass and all—I still had to fork out $3,500. I thought at least I'd get to keep the old pump as a memento.

For the next two weeks I wore the sling, but I'd go over to Edie's and have my kids lift up my right arm to stretch it. I'm thinking it's tight from the accident, but after the two weeks are over and I really can't lift it up more than ten inches, I go back to the doctor. When I see him, I say, "Hey, I'm no puss, but I'm really having a hard time with this arm." Well, they X-ray the shoulder only to find I have a clean break in the arm about eight inches from the shoulder just below where the upper muscle attaches to the arm. So every time I tried to lift it, it was actually pulling the break apart.

Now that I know it's not in my head, I just let it go, even though the doctor suggested putting in pins. I keep the arm immobile for six more weeks, and it healed okay. I think I'd have to be run over by a semi while being chased by the Alphabet Squad to have a worse day.

CHAPTER 21

GUIDANCE COUNSELOR'S NIGHTMARE

I've been more than a drug dealer, pimp, and bill collector—over my lifetime I've had a lot of different jobs. I guess the first one was selling these little yarn dolls my mother made when we lived in the projects after my dad got hurt. The whole family pitched in to help. Mom would make up a bunch and wrap them in pairs, then I'd go downtown to sell them at Christmastime. I was about ten years old, and I did so good it paid for Christmas that first year—Mom said I could sell ice to an Eskimo.

I also did a lot of shoe shining with my brother Billy. We had a set route—the Jackson Buffet, the Poodle Dog (home of the Giant Double), the Viaduct, and Sugar's. I must have been about ten when I started, and I was really good. In addition to the shoe shining, I even helped set bowling pins at Harken's in Saint Paul.

After that, we moved to Cottage Grove. My first job there was in the summer, working for a neighbor who owned Coreless Landscaping. I worked in the sod fields rolling the sod after it was cut. Boy, that job sucked. Then I got a job at Ryan's Landscaping where my dad drove a truck. I was on a sod crew and moved my way up to a crew that planted trees along I-35 from Saint Paul to Rochester. I was sixteen and the youngest, but I partied with them for most of the summer. It all ended when we were supposed to lay the front lawns of a new housing project. We were about half shot on wine, and someone decided it would be faster if we just started at one end, spread the sod to the other end, and then cut in the driveways and sidewalks afterward. Well, let me say that when Art, the owner, showed up and saw the sod laid over everything, the shit hit the fan and we were all fired on the spot.

The next job I got was selling women's shoes at the Golden Rule in downtown Saint Paul. What a job for a sixteen-year-old!—business was looking up, we used to say. That lasted for about a month, and then I went to Dayton's to sell women's shoes there. I didn't fit in, and that lasted three weeks. So I ended up at this factory that made paintbrush handles. I worked in the lacquer room, where I dipped the handles to give them the red, white, and blue tips. That lasted two months, and then I went to Volama Company, where I ran a punch press cutting out racing stripes for about one and a half months. I also worked for Day Appliance for about two hours—I was a stock man and had to fill orders from three floors of parts. No way!

Then there was Ideal Brass and Security, where I worked with two of my drinking buddies, Randy Bowman and Bob Davis. They would pick me up in the morning with two cases of beer and two bottles of Four Roses whiskey in the car so we'd be ready for work. From punching in to punching out, we were always shitfaced. This went on for about three months until I spilled a box of 3,000 aluminum screen door knobs down three flights of stairs. The racket lasted for about twenty minutes—I was fired, believe it or not.

So I showed up back at the employment office where I had gotten all the other jobs. The management said they saw a pattern developing and put me in this class for the hard-to-employ. After that, I was sent to be a guard at the State Capitol, where I helped move a bunch of old state law books to a new location. I soon learned those tunnels and rooms were a great place to hide and drink. That job lasted one month, until they found me sleeping with a bottle of Old Crow in my hand.

Then I worked at Standard Battery, U.S. Gypsum, Gopher Lead and Smelting, Henley's Furniture, and Gould Battery. Actually, "worked" is quite a loose term. I was employed at Gould for about six years, five of which I spent on Workmen's Compensation. The first time it was for a broken left hand, which I smashed in the mast of a forklift while working in the warehouse. I broke every bone in my hand and pushed one knuckle out the palm, so I was off for one year. Then I got back to work just before a strike. I wasn't real popular because while on Comp I went into the office to pick up a check, and while there I had a misunderstanding with the head of personnel. I overreacted to him telling me I should learn to work with my "little owie" by chasing him around the office saying I was going to give him a "little owie." Management tried to fire me, but they couldn't because I was on Comp. Then they figured they were going to get even during the strike by giving me all the shit picket duties. As luck would have it, as I was walking through the warehouse back to my workstation, I caught, so to speak, a truck battery that was falling off a conveyer line and injured my back. I had to be taken out on a gurney, and off to the hospital I went with a back injury. Back on Comp, too bad.

Next, I was a recreation director for two years at Phalen

Youth Club and never missed a day, but I was on a CETA grant and the money ran out. After that I opened an antique shop where Edie and Jessica did a lot of the fleamarkets and auctions with me. That was really good income for about three years. After that, I tried computer programming and went to school at Globe, but it wasn't for me.

Finally, I went to Saint Paul Technical College to learn auto mechanics. I thought I'd found my niche, but I got in trouble because I had a towing service at the same time, and I got caught because I'd run an ad for mechanic work that said they should drop off the cars to be worked on at my house. Then I'd bring them down to the school and have the students fix them. One time, a teacher couldn't get his car into the shop because we were so backed up, so he answered the ad. When he saw his car in the jam-up at the school, the jig was up, and I had a choice of quitting or being expelled. I quit.

All this led to a mechanic's job at a motorcycle shop. I'd never really worked on bikes before, but I figured, how hard can it be? That weekend I got some Harley manuals and did a lot of reading. By Tuesday, I did my first top-end job, and it held together. I picked all the stuff up really fast, so about two months into it, I figured it was about time I got paid. This seemed to come as a shock to Guts, the guy who owned the shop with his partner, Dave. They had a quick meeting and asked me if I wanted to be a partner. Sure, why not? So I was half owner of Iron Horse Engineering in Saint Paul Park.

This went on for about a year when I decided to open my own shop. I found a nice building across the river in South Saint Paul, and I had it stocked and ready in about a month (with a little secret help from the Iron Horse account). So off I went. I guess I should have told Guts and Dave because after a week they called me to see where I'd been, and I told them about Deadeye's Custom Cycle. They took it really well and wished me luck—they had no idea they'd financed my endeavor. The shop went well until the bust, then business fell off, so I moved it up to Western and University and sold it to Butch.

About now I figured I'd go to school to be a chef—I've always liked food—just in case I got busted. That way I could end up working in the kitchen where the food and yeast are, and all the other necessities for a good life. I enrolled in T.V.I. Hotel and Restaurant Cookery and learned I was really good at this cooking thing. (I also picked up about twenty-five new customers for my drug business on the side.) I got almost all the way through the course and then quit to be a broiler chef at a four-star Italian restaurant in Saint Paul. I lasted about four months there because my work schedule interfered with my drug business, so I quit.

Then something new happened in the business line. I was walking past a gallery one day and saw a Bev Doolittle print. I had to have it. I got to know the owner (Jim Bowen) well, and when he saw I was really interested and had money to invest, he gave me a crash course in print sales. I dove right in, and before I knew it, I started my own print shop business—Eye of the Beholder. The business was good, and I got to meet a lot of interesting people, including several artists like Robert Olsen and Bev Doolittle. Also, my looks were a help (I was a little rough-edged) when I'd go to other galleries shopping. I'd play dumb, and they'd give me a really good deal. I was always on the lookout at

the out-of-state galleries like in Vegas or Memphis. All this went on until things cooled off in the print business, and I pulled out. I managed to get rid of all my stock, though.

When my second marriage (to Lisa) was falling apart (even though I didn't know it), I picked up some much-needed cash running two kitchens. Then I took over Pat's Pub on Dale and Minnehaha, which went okay until several locals jumped one of my club brothers after I'd gone home. They were shown the error of their ways about a week later. When he found out, Pat said, "We can't have people get beaten with bats because it's not good for business."

"Oh well, shit happens," I replied, and found myself unemployed again.

Somehow, though, I never stayed unemployed long. I started a taco place at Bugg's—Dos Amigos—and then managed Coachman's Pub on Dale and Maryland. Friends helped me cook and manage, and things were booming. I even had some other-worldly approval (I'm not sure it was approval, exactly). One night I was getting to know one of the waitresses when I heard this crash. I ran downstairs, but nothing was there. Then another time I saw someone standing by the front door after hours. I approached really slow with my fist all ready to blast him, but the entryway was empty and the door locked. One of the regulars told me that several years ago an off-duty cop had shot and killed a robber right in the doorway. The hair stood up on my neck, and I began to lose fondness for the place. Then several months later on a Saturday night, we were having a wedding party for Brother Speedo when some kids tried to crash it, got thrown out, and came back with guns and shot up the place. Dick Fallhaber, an old club member, got shot six times with a 9-millimeter, but he lived. The kids went to jail.

Business fell off after that, and I decided to spend the winter in Vegas. I thought I'd just get a cooking job there, but I ended up being a repo man for a guy who paid me $100 a car. I usually did six to eight cars a week, enough for rent and gambling money. That went on for four years—winter in Vegas collecting cars, summers in Saint Paul working the counter in Butch's Custom.

Finally I ended up with what was probably my best cooking job ever. A kitchen was for rent at the Roseville V.F.W., and my old food sales rep, Al Grizinski, who kept in touch after I left Dos Amigos, told me about it. He was a great guy who always was trying to get me back cooking. I thought I'd just check it out, and who did I meet there but Karla Miller, one of my favorite people and one of their bartenders. She told Marv, the manager, that he had to hire me. In the end, I said I'd let them know, though I was already packed for Vegas.

Then I found out my sister Sue and her husband wanted to sell the duplex they owned with my mom, who didn't want to move. Before I knew it, I made a deal with them to buy them out so my mom could stay, and I ended up moving into the first floor. That meant I'd be anchored in Minnesota, so I accepted the job at the V.F.W.

As it turned out, all things worked out better than I'd expected. Mom got to stay where she wanted, and Edie and Jessica ended up moving into the first floor about a year later, and I moved into the furnished basement. The job at the Roseville V.F.W. was one of the best experiences I've ever had with the people I came to know and love—like Dawn, the little old lady who was a mainstay at the place. (The first words she said to me were, "We're not happy about an outsider coming in and taking over the kitchen.")

Within two weeks, she ended up being one of my strongest supporters. And then there was John and Karla, Carol and Bob, Olga, Chris, and Sue M., my wife in my next life—along with all the other great people who accepted and took in a long-haired, tattooed biker as one of their own.

CHAPTER 22

THE TRICKSTER

I've always been known for my sense of humor, but it has gotten me in trouble a lot of times. Like the time I was over visiting my old friend Dave. He and Sue had just had a baby about nine months earlier, and Dave was taking care of little Sally while his wife was out shopping. He was changing her, and that made me think of a great trick to play on his wife. As luck would have it, they had a can of refried beans, so I got a new diaper and put some beans on it and smushed it together. Then we put it on the side of the changing table and waited.

When Sue got home, we chatted awhile in the living room until Dave said he would change the baby again before we took off. Well, we went in her room and killed some time until his wife came in. Then Dave changed Sally and put the real diaper next to the one with the beans. I said, "Boy, that sure smells strange."

She said, "No, that's normal for babies."

"Let me see the diaper," I said.

She got this surprised and disgusted look on her face as Dave gave me the fake diaper and I was examining it. (I made sure it was the one with the beans—I didn't really trust old Dave not to nail me.) As I held it up to my face to look at the deposit, Sue was looking at me like I had three heads. "What are you feeding this kid?" I asked.

She replied, "Just normal Heinz baby food." Well, I gave it a good sniff, then took a bite out of it. She lost it, screamed, and started puking—she was white as a ghost.

We got her settled down and told her what we did, but she saw *noooo* humor in it, and old Dave was grounded. I figured I'd better leave. I still get roars when I tell people about that one.

Another friend of mine, Ralph, and his new girlfriend had just moved into their new house, and Ralph and I decided to pull a housewarming trick on her. It started out with Ralph saying, "What's that noise?" as we were sitting in the den.

I said, "I think it could be mice." Well, she pulled her feet up into the fetal position on the couch, saying that she couldn't stand mice. We made these listening gestures throughout the evening, and Ralph kept it up for several days.

A few days later I was invited over for dinner. She had several girlfriends over, too. Before I got there, I stopped at a pet store and picked up the biggest rat they had and put it in my jacket pocket.

Everyone was in the den when I arrived, and Ralph had mentioned the noises several times already, according to our plan. When I came in, he said, "Let's hang up your coat in the den closet." When we got to the closet, he said, "Do you hear that?" We started rutting around inside, I got the rat out of my pocket, and came out with it in my hand. There was these three women sitting on the couch, all with their feet tucked up under them, and holding hands. When they saw the rat, a scream rose, the likes of which I have never heard.

It pierced my ears and made me drop the rat. He was in escape mode and headed for the safety of the couch bottom. I swear the three of them levitated off the couch, hung there for about a minute, and literally ran through the air for the safety of the kitchen.

Ralph and I dropped into pools of laughing shit. We couldn't move, we were laughing so hard. Finally after about five minutes of us laughing and crying and the women screaming and huddling in the kitchen, we composed ourselves enough to go on the rat hunt because we knew the women wouldn't settle down and there would be utter chaos until the rat was found.

After about an hour of moving furniture and chasing the poor guy, we finally cornered it and put it in a pillowcase, trying not to hurt it. I took it out to my truck and put it in a box. (Later I gave it to a friend's kid who liked animals.) I don't know who was more upset, the rat or the women.

Several days later, Ralph told his wife what we'd done. I didn't see him for about a month, and when I did meet him at a bar, he told me I'd better lay low because all three women had sworn a pact to get even with me. Which they did, by coming up to me when I was with a date and saying, "Thanks for giving us the clap." That was a real buzzkill. They also started several nasty rumors, including coming up to me once and saying, "You could at least come by and see your baby once in a while." But I lived through it.

Then I remember another time when I was prospecting for the Spokesmen, and I set up a joke with Pitso after he asked me if I could still get hand grenades. I said, "Yes," and he said he wanted one. So for about three weeks he would always ask me about the grenade, and all the club members heard about it.

Finally, at our meeting, there were about eight of us bikers in the front room. Pitso said again, "Did you get the grenade?"

I said, "Yes, it's $25."

Pitso said, "Great, give it to me." So I pulled it out of my jacket. Everyone was interested in this new acquisition.

As they were all looking, I held it out in my hand and said, "$25." Pitso said he'd pay me later. According to plan, then, I pulled back my hand with the grenade—I was holding it so Pitso could reach for it and grab the pin. But I had put a spring under the spoon so when the pin came out, the spoon would fly across the room.

What happened next was even better than I could have imagined. The grenade hit the floor, and everyone just freaked. I mean, one jumped behind the couch, two almost killed each other trying to get out the door at the same time, one ran right into the wall, I mean like in the cartoons. One dived right out the window through the screen. It was hilarious—they were all beat-up and bruised. Of course I ended up holding the short end of the shit stick, but it was worth it all. I still think back about it and laugh.

With these tricks, a lot of people don't know if I'm pulling their leg or not. Once on a run, we had this hangaround named Tom with us—he'd lost his leg in a bike accident, but they'd done such a great job on his fake leg that, shit, I didn't even know until he mentioned it to me. Several people came back to the campsite to party, and all of a sudden I got this idea for a great prank. I talked to Tom about it, and we agreed to pull their legs.

At about 4 a.m., Tom said he was tired and wanted to go crash. He went to his tent, and after about twenty minutes, I said, "What a bunch of shit. He's just a party pooper. I'm going to teach him a lesson and pull him out of that tent." Then I went to get some rope. I pushed my bike over by his tent and tied the rope to the sissy bar. Then I unzipped his tent, exposing his feet. (Tom had agreed to have his leg on real loose and to cut his pants leg about halfway up.)

Well, I tied the rope on the ankle of his fake leg (after I'd made sure I had the right one!) and had Micky start up my bike. When I signalled, he took off to pull Tom out of the tent. The bike took off with the boot and leg trailing behind, with Tom, still in the tent, screaming and moaning, "My leg! My leg!"

I mean it was hilarious. There were eight people standing there in total shock watching the leg bouncing at the end of the rope like a bad water skier. Shit, one girl passed out. People were screaming and carrying on like it was the end of the world. I mean, they woke everyone up. People were scrambling out of their tents half naked. It was a Kodak moment. Then I heard Butch yell, "Deadeye!" and I made myself scarce for about an hour until everyone saw the humor.

One of the best tricks I ever played, though, was when I was bouncing at Bugg's. These three guys there were real pains in my ass, but they were the kind I couldn't just beat up. All three of them together would add up to one-half of a good fight, and I would just come off looking like a bully.

I was wondering how I could straighten them out when I thought of getting a transvestite to do it for me. Well, that's not something you need every day, so I did some checking around. I knew a lot of people and could find anything I needed. It ended up I had a customer who was a cross dresser. (I had no idea at first.) He introduced me to several trannys, and I picked out this guy who was better looking than some of the girls I had been out with. I couldn't tell

anything was going on even though I knew. He (I'll just call him "he" after this) was about six feet tall with long blond hair, 36-23-38 measurements, and a voice like a girl's. I mean, he could have fooled anyone except for the one thing.

I told Steve, which was his name, what I wanted to do, and we settled on a price. I had to guarantee he'd make it out of there safe, though. All this happened on a Monday night, and when Friday rolled around, he showed up at the bar in a denim shirt and bra and a matching skirt. I mean, when he walked in, all heads turned. When he ordered a drink, four different guys offered to pay.

He looked around and recognized the Three Stooges from a picture I had given him. He walked around, played the jukebox, and finally went to the women's bathroom near where they were. When he walked by, he smiled, and sure as shit, one of them said something to him when he came out, so he joined them. Everyone at the bar was wondering why the hell this lovely woman was sitting with these turds.

As the night progressed (and several 7-7s later), they started to fool around. They were pressing up against him and taking turns rubbing his ass. Finally the kissing started. They were all getting into the act. The people around the bar were amazed—was this being nice to shitheads in a parallel universe?

As closing time got closer, I came up near them when I mentioned to several people that there was a party I was going to after closing. As planned, Steve said, "Hey, can we come?"

I said, "Sure, why not?"

Well, with the drinks and all the ass rubbing, titty bumping, and Steve rubbing their special spots, it couldn't have been going better, and at closing time about eight people from the bar, plus Steve and his new friends, were off to the party. Steve told them he had to take his car because he didn't want to leave it at the bar.

They were all upset, saying, "You're coming to the party, aren't you?"

He said, "For sure."

Soon we got to the party, and the guys were the hit with all their kissing and carrying on. Eventually they all took turns going into the bedroom, and each one came out bragging about how great she was—they had never had such great head. She really knew what a man wanted. Well, I might say everyone was quite impressed.

After they were all done, we were all just sitting around. Then Steve said, "You guys had your fun, now how about me?" They started in about how they were going to take care of her, so he stands up, lifts up his skirt, and pulls out about nine inches of manhood. I swear the world stopped for about a minute—everyone just sat still or stood there in shock. I mean, they didn't even blink. (Steve took that as his cue to leave.) I think it was at least five minutes before anyone even moved.

Then the real shit started. "Whoa, dudes, that was a guy—you got a blow job from a guy and you weren't even in jail!—no wonder he knew what a guy likes." It went on and on.

Well, we didn't see much of the trio after that. One wife found out about it, and that poor schmuck was in his "not doing anything except working and going home" mode.

CHAPTER 23

HOME SWEET HOME

Any biker club worth anything has a clubhouse. It's a place where the guys can hang out and relax. The club members pay for it one way or another and keep it up. Biker clubs are nonprofit organizations a lot of times, like the Masons or the Boy Scouts. Well, maybe not just like them.

The Los Valientes Motorcycle Club was started in 1976 by twenty-two bikers. The first actual clubhouse we had, we got from Tooter when he was going to move from the East Side on Sixth Street just down from Sacred Heart Church out to Stacey. Then, about ten years ago, we bought a beat-up duplex on Western Avenue in Saint Paul. We all chipped in for the down payment. It was all ours. When we knew that its street address was 666, we never had any doubt that it was meant for us.

The brothers fixed it up, built a bar, brought in two refrigerators for beer and pop, got a nice big table for playing cards, a TV and stereo, sofas, and several La-Z-Boy recliners. Upstairs were two bedrooms, so if anyone needed a place to crash, he could. We never had to ask "Where's the party?" because it was always at the Los Valientes clubhouse, and it lasted as long as we did. Nobody was there to bitch us out or complain about having to go to work in the morning. Because of the prospects doing their duties, it was always clean and stocked with beer. We held all our meetings there. "Going to church" is what bikers call their meetings, and we were a pretty religious bunch.

A lot of people can't understand the brotherhood bikers feel. Maybe it's because they see us as violent. The lifestyle we choose to live means bike accidents and fighting just to stand up for what we believe in. But for me, if I call someone a brother, it means that that person would go to the wall for me, no questions asked, and I would do the same for him, no hesitation. I believe that family is the strongest bond—parents to kids, kids to parents, siblings to each other. But our true brotherhood is just as strong, if not stronger in some areas. You are born into a regular family, and you have each other unconditionally, where in a club you choose to be with one another, and that choice has a lot of power.

There have been days when I just would say, "No more, that's it." Then I'd go to the clubhouse and run into Butch or Mongo or Tommy, and after ten minutes I'd forget what I was all twisted up about. The brotherhood only works because it is founded in true friendship, not because of money or power trips.

I remember that once we had a brother whose name was Doc. He'd had a stroke, and after he got out of the hospital, the doctor wanted him to go to a nursing home. Well, we said, "No way—he's family, and you take care of family." He also was a diabetic, and we all learned about his medication so we could help him with it. He moved into the clubhouse, and we always had a club member with him. At the parties,

runs, and meetings, someone was always stopping in to see him. We also used to sneak candy bars to him—he wasn't supposed to have them, but he liked them so much.

Doc lived for three years, and finally his heart gave out. His real brother came down for his body, and he told us he couldn't believe how much we'd cared for Doc. But that's what it's about. The house has always been there for brothers who needed a safe haven or were down on their luck, including myself. They always had a place to stay and eat, because we take care of our own.

The Los Valientes have a lot of retired members—brothers who aren't required to attend the meetings and go on the runs anymore, but who can use the clubhouse and be a part of things. You can retire after seven years' membership. I was a retired member, but I came back to full membership, and now I'm club president. We're all still around and will be for a long time to come.

A lot of people ask me what a normal night at the clubhouse would be like. I think, What's normal? but here goes.

I walk in about 7 p.m. to some Willie Nelson or maybe some Stray Cats on the stereo, and there's Dick in front of the slot, and he yells, "Hey, Boss," and I look over behind the bar where prospects Harlen or Brent are bartending, and Dominic and Polack are hanging around talking about a run that's coming up, and they look up and say, "Hi, Deadeye."

Someone asks me what I want to drink, and I settle down in one of the La-Z-Boys, and maybe Gale and his wife Terry walk in, and he starts bitching about his tattoo shop, and Terry just laughs. Mother Mick is sitting there watching the History Channel about the wild West, and Bill asks him if he recognizes anyone, and he grumbles, "Eat me."

Then we hear three or four bikes racing down Western,

and we can tell one of them is Tommy's Boss Hoss 375 Horse with a 100-HP nitrous boost. Only Tommy could ride that, and he does. I walk out to greet everyone, and someone yells, "Let's get a card game going and get some of Deadeye's money!" (I never win—I think if I did, it would be one of the seven signs for the end of the world.) We start playing with maybe a $10–$20 buy-in, and people keep showing up. Burp and Ryan hang around—they're great guys. The conversation goes from old runs to new runs, and maybe Dominic comes up with a shit story, and someone mentions stopping by the Lamplighter after the card game.

That's what it's about—just people hanging 'n' doing what they want to do and enjoying the time we spend with each other. Riding, drinking, bullshitting, that's what it's about, enjoying who you are and what you do. The Word According to Deadeye.

CHAPTER 24

BLINDED BY THE LIGHT

I **think** I have a pretty good memory for all the things that have happened in my life, but occasionally something just jumps out at you. It's like it comes through your skin as well as your head, even after years have passed. I feel that way about the time I met the future ex–Mrs. Hayes who was to become my second wife.

I was visiting a girl who was both a friend and a customer, and there was this gorgeous five-foot-nine blonde with big eyes, a smile that would melt your heart, and a great ass. Terry, my friend, introduced us, and I fell in lust with Lisa right then. I kept seeing her around after that, and I kept checking with Terry on her status—it turned out she was engaged to another guy I knew. But one thing led to another, and when I found out that we both liked country music (I was a real Conway Twitty and George Jones fan, and they were coming to town), I asked her to the concert. She said she was engaged and didn't think that would be right. I backed off.

Then I found out she wasn't exactly happy with her current situation, and Terry set up a night when I could take Lisa out just to show her there was something else out there.

Terry also told me that Lisa was only nineteen. I was thirty-eight, but I didn't look, act, or feel thirty-eight, and I couldn't have cared less. I took her out for something to eat and a couple drinks, then asked her if she liked to play slot machines. She said, "Sure," so we went to the clubhouse and played for a couple hours at the slots in the basement.

The night wasn't over, though. We went upstairs to the front room to watch TV. Before I knew it, we'd started kissing, and then all hell broke loose. After four or five hours (I wasn't looking at my watch) and the destruction of one couch, one end table, one coffee table, two lamps, and some pictures, one of my club brothers from upstairs came down to see what the hell was going on. When he saw us, he just said, "Oh, sorry!" and left us alone as fast as he could.

When Lisa finally got ready to go home, I saw that her back was bleeding—the worst rug burn I ever saw. I thought, What the hell is she going to tell her fiancé? But I left that to her and dropped her off at Terry's. All the drive home I kept thinking about the night's events—it was the kind of thing guys brag about to their friends or write about to *Playboy*. For me, though, it wasn't just the raw, primal sex (though there had been plenty of that), but more the connection I felt—it was like I'd come alive again, and I was hooked.

I didn't see Lisa for a week (she said she had to rest and heal her back). She'd told her fiancé she'd slipped on the stairs. That was the longest week ever—it was like when you are about to get out of jail and just counting the seconds, swearing someone is setting back the clock.

When I did see her, I got a limo and brought her diamond earrings, nice ones, about one-half carat each. This time we didn't break any furniture, but you could say we christened that limousine.

Then two days later I met Lisa and her fiancé when I was taking my two daughters to a movie. He was wearing one of the diamond studs in his ear. I didn't say a word, just went with him to look at the new speakers in his car and introduced him to Jessica and Danielle. I was sneaking glances at Lisa and smiling, thinking of our time together. I didn't even mind about her sharing the earrings.

It was no surprise that Lisa and I kept seeing each other. I couldn't imagine it any other way. After several dates, she decided to stay over at my place in Forest Lake. We listened to Conway Twitty and finally decided it was time for a little shut-eye. As she went to lay down, her head hit something hard under the passenger pillow. I had forgot that I had a sawed-off shotgun under it, as well as a 357 on my side of the bed between the water mattress and the sideboard. She gave me a funny look, but I just said, "It's in case the bogeyman shows up."

Actually, I don't think Lisa had any idea of who or what I was. She didn't know that just three weeks before, I'd been up for four to seven days running, high on coke, and then sleeping for three. She didn't know that, until I met her, my ritual upon waking was to lay there staring at the ceiling, saying, "Another shitty day," then reaching over, grabbing the 357, taking out five of the six shells, cocking back the hammer, spinning the cylinder, putting the gun to my head and pulling the trigger. I'd done that for three months, expecting every time that I'd be finished with everything, but the cylinder always hit an empty chamber. She didn't know how low and lonely a person can be, with the dark emptiness inside so bad it's actually physical pain. Not happy, not sad, just hollow. Money, drugs, possessions didn't mean shit. But all of a sudden I was looking at her while she slept and not believing how happy I was. There was Lisa next to me. How was it possible to go from that darkness into the light she brought? I was like a little kid, and every day was Christmas.

Over the next week, Lisa stayed over several times, and then finally she was staying all the time. I don't think we left the house for a month except to get groceries. We sat for hours kissing and talking, then making love. My drug use ceased—I didn't want anything to rob me of every second I could spend with her. I did persuade her to call her mom so they wouldn't report her missing. When she did, her family was relieved, but they wanted to know what the hell was going on. Who could blame them?

Finally I dropped her off at her house—actually a few houses away for safety's sake. Then I went to take care of business, which I had been letting go ever since I started getting involved with her. I'd even neglected my duties with the club. The only one who knew anything about my situation was Butch, and he just said that I seemed in a good mood.

After several days, Lisa called and asked me to pick her up. I was there like a shot. We came back to my place and had a serious talk. I let her know exactly how I felt about her, and she said she felt the same—she'd even broken up with her fiancé, but she was worried about repercussions. I reassured her by telling her that he would get over it, though all the time I was thinking if I was in his position, I would have moved mountains to get her back.

Well, she moved in with me for good. I was still letting my drug business go to shit, and I knew I had to settle that. I had a sit-down with the people above me and told them I was getting out for a while because I was way too hot. Usually a dealer doesn't make a decision like this on his own, but I was in solid with them, and they were agreeable. They just asked

me if I knew anyone I could vouch for to take my place, but I just said "No"—I'd seen what being in that position could do, and I wasn't going to put my ass on the line by having someone I'd recommended screw up. After several drinks, we parted, and they told me to come back any time I wanted.

All of this was good in a lot of ways. First Lisa had been my savior, getting me out of the depression I was in and turning my life around. Then several of the people I was dealing with got busted, and one of my best friends died of liver cancer, which had probably been brought on by the crank. It was like a new chapter beginning in my life.

Then I finally got to meet Lisa's family, starting with her aunt Kelly, who is a knockout brunette and a drug counselor. I met Lisa's mother and her brothers Seth, Shane, and Russ. Then I met Kelly's husband, Bill, who turned out to be a really good friend. Not everything was perfect, though—Lisa's stepdad, a bad ass from Saint Paul Park who knew about me, told her mom that they would end up finding Lisa dead in a ditch if she stayed with me. I made several calls to inform him that he must be psychic, but he envisioned the wrong person in the ditch. No more was said about that.

It was really great how Lisa's family, overall, accepted me. They knew there was something not quite right about me even beyond the age difference, but they knew I cared about their daughter. Lisa was happy, and that was what counted.

Now we started our whole life together. I figured I had a little over a million dollars cash stashed away, and that ought to last forever. I indulged her with trips to Vegas and all kinds of shopping. She'd never had a nice car, and she didn't like to drive my Benz because it made her nervous, so I said

I'd get her whatever she wanted. She wanted a Corvette, so out we went shopping. We found a nice low-miles burgundy one with all the trimmings, and as luck would have it, I knew the salesman and got a smoking deal. I didn't think life could get better than it was for us.

As part of all this, we decided to get married, and we just did it on one of our trips to Vegas. But Lisa wanted a big wedding later, so we set the date and started planning after we got back. I'd kind of forgotten that I was still married to Edie, so I had to get that taken care of, too, and then because we were Catholic and wanted a Catholic wedding, I had to get an annulment of my first marriage from the church. That was a little harder to do, but I was persistent, and that got done, as well.

Somewhere in here Lisa had a miscarriage. She wanted kids and felt real bad about it. I did, too, but figured we had plenty of time for that and everything would work itself out.

Next was where we were going to live. Lisa wanted a bigger house so my daughters and her brothers could stay over with us. So we started shopping for houses (an area in which I have some expertise), and we found one on Flowerfield in Lexington. When I walked into the entryway, I said, "We'll take it" before I even looked farther inside. It was a four-bedroom split with a fireplace in the lower level, and it was perfect.

Lisa was in seventh heaven what with the house and the wedding plans. We found a priest in Blaine who wasn't too hung up on our age difference, and we went to marriage classes. We even took a compatibility test and got the highest score he'd ever seen. Then came the wedding, and it was beautiful with all the bridesmaids and groomsmen. I had some of my club brothers up from our chapter in New

Mexico, along with the brothers from our club here in Saint Paul. We had the reception at the Withrow Ballroom, which was packed. It was one hell of a party, and people still talk about it—I think they should for what it cost me.

After that we settled into married life. Almost right away I found this great house in Forest Lake by Scandia. It was like our own country—ten acres, four bedrooms, a fenced in-ground pool, a pole barn, a 300-foot driveway with a pond and trees on each side so it was like going through a tunnel to drive up. The front yard even had a gazebo. The neighbors on one side raised deer and peacocks (I found out that peacocks are really noisy), and the neighbors on the other side were blocked off by the trees. We moved in as fast as we could and rented the house on Flowerfield to a club brother, his wife, their two kids, and a very large Rottweiler that weighed about 160 pounds.

We moved into our Garden of Eden and everything was happy. Then about four months later, while I had been at a club meeting and Lisa was with her grandparents, I drove up the driveway only to see that the house was on fire. I called the fire department, but they couldn't find the place right away, so I stood in the rain, hearing the sirens go by on the road and watching my house burn to the ground.

This all led to trouble with the fire marshall, who wanted to see my income tax returns for the last four years, and with the insurance company, who were in no hurry to settle. It was a real Pandora's box. We were homeless, too, because the Flowerfield house was rented. We ended up renting a town house before I could get the Flowerfield house back.

That's when the money started to run low, so I decided I'd better go back to work. I had a friend set me up with a deal that would make me about ten grand, but when I was leaving to go see him, Lisa started yakking about how I should return the movies we'd rented that were late, and how I ought to do it right away. I wasn't happy because I ended up a half hour late as I turned onto 35th Avenue from Hiawatha by my friend's place. It looked like he was having a used car sale in his yard. I thought, What the hell? and then I realized that it was a raid, and that if I'd been on time, I'd have been walking out with a quarter L.B. of crank in my pocket.

This was kind of a turning point for me. I went home and told Lisa I was going to get a real job. "Who'd hire you?" was the first thing she said. I took that as a challenge, and by two o'clock the next day, I was running the kitchen at Macalusa's on Pierce Butler Route. After about six months, the place was sold and they let everyone go, but I was out of work for only about a week when I took over the kitchen at the All American on Century.

During this time, we didn't do much traveling or shopping because I had to actually work for my money. Lisa was getting restless, so she waitressed at the restaurant for a while, but that didn't work out. Then she went to work for this telemarketer. The more I worked, the more distant she got, and then about six months later, on my birthday, my mother dropped into the restaurant with my gift and card. She left, then came back a little later. "There's something I've got to tell you," she said.

That was when it all ended. My mother told me that Lisa had hooked up with this Puerto Rican crackhead. My brother Joe lived just two houses from the crackhead's place, and word had moved through the rest of my family real fast. It was hard to miss a five-foot-nine blonde in a burgundy Vette.

Although I probably should have known something was going on, I was completely blindsided. Things weren't the same as they'd been in the beginning, but then nothing is. I hadn't suspected a thing. I tore out of the restaurant and drove out to find her, thinking that love must not only be blind, but dumb, too. It was a good thing it took me twenty minutes to get to her aunt's house where she was, because I needed that much time to cool down.

At least Lisa was honest about what had gone on—when I confronted her, she admitted to the indiscretion. Over the next days, I tried to work things out with her, but she had no intention of doing anything different. She ended up moving to her aunt's house in Minneapolis, where I visited her a couple of times a week. I knew she was going through a tough time, and I wanted to help her. I'd take her out to eat and talk, but after a little while, she just said right out, "I never loved you and never will. But I knew you'd take care of me." To this day, I still try to tell myself that she was just saying that to make me move on.

After all this, I was devastated. But there was nothing I could do. Things marched on, and we filed for divorce, and bankruptcy, too. We agreed that I'd give her $5,000 and her jewelry and her favorite prints, and that I wouldn't kill her boyfriend. About then, I found out that he'd been arrested for driving without a license and with crack in his pocket, and that he was probably going to do time. I thought, Great, I have a lot of friends in Stillwater Prison. I'll have them fill his dance card, and when he gets out he'll be more interested in her brothers than in her.

We had a lot of hassle getting things settled because Lisa kept wanting more stuff and the judge was screwing around. I actually snuck the divorce through while Lisa wasn't there because she thought the hearing had been postponed. We had a big fight about the Vette, and when she came to the storage place with two police officers, to get it, it wasn't there. (I wonder what happened.) She came unglued and wanted to charge me with auto theft. The police officers got involved, and then some suits showed up and started talking about what an asshole I was and how she wouldn't be safe unless I was in prison. Lisa said all she knew about me was that I made great tacos! Even though she was still so pissed, she called me up to let me know what was going on.

On another occasion, she and her boyfriend (he didn't go to prison after all) got a place, and I offered to move some of the things she had left behind over there for her. I picked her up and brought her out to our house so she could show me what she wanted. When she started, shit, I never saw so many shoes and boots in my life outside of a shoe store.

While she was hauling out stuff, I was listening to Bob Seger. I purposely put on "Somewhere Tonight" just to get a reaction out of her. (It had been one of our favorites.) But no luck.

Lisa and me loaded up everything—clothes, shoes, prints, futon—and started out for her house. She was acting really down, and I thought maybe she would change her mind even now. So I asked her what was wrong, and she just looked at me all sad. I thought, Maybe she misses me.

Then she just said, "You know what's wrong."

My heartbeat picked up, and I thought, Okay, she is missing me, and she does want to get back together. (It's strange how stupid love makes you.)

Everything was quiet. Then, after several minutes, she looked up and said, "I really miss my Corvette."

Talk about a wake-up call! I was just reeling and couldn't

say a thing. Then Conway Twitty came on doing "I Want to Know You," which was our wedding song.

She chirps, "Our song!"

I shot back, "That's not our song anymore."

So she says, "What is?"

All I could think of was AC/DC's "Giving a Dog a Bone." She saw no humor in my selection. Tough shit.

When we got to her house, I told her I would put everything out in the yard, because I wouldn't step foot into the little love nest. I couldn't guarantee my actions. She said her boyfriend was at work, but I didn't care. Then, after we had everything unloaded in the front yard, who comes to the door but Mr. Crackhead. He said, "You'd better get out of here and never come around again!" That turd—my money that I gave Lisa was what was used to get this place, not one dime of his. He said, "If you don't go now, I'll kick your ass." Neat—if he wanted to party, I was all for it.

I said, "Why wait?—let's do it now." Right away he jumped inside and started yelling at me through the door.

My instinct was to go after him, and I did. But as I got to the door, I thought, This guy is a little chickenshit—why is he so pumped up? I happened to turn around, and sure as hell, there were two squad cars just around the corner watching the whole thing. That shit had called the cops, and there they were waiting for me to be me so they could witness the whole thing. I don't think that dipshit realized they would have just sat there till I was done with him just to get more charges on me like Forced Entry and probably Attempted Murder or worse by the time I got done.

Well, someone was watching out for me. I just gave him the finger and left them to their little love shack. A lot of people were surprised why I never went after him. But I gave my word—and deep down, I knew Lisa would chew him up and spit him out. He seemed like the kind of person who would go off the deep end and probably turn himself into a piñata, hanging from a rafter. Too bad, too sad.

After that, I had to figure out how to live my life without Lisa. I thought about using again, even bought coke a couple of times. I remember picking up an eight-ball from the table and squeezing it—Conway Twitty was singing, and I was just about ready to start in again. But I didn't. I guess I figured I'd come out the other side of something and I might as well stay there.

In a year or so, Lisa cooled off and we became regular friends. When she needed a break from her boyfriend, she'd come over. I remember one particular weekend when she stayed with me. On Monday morning, I reached for the phone and dialed her number. When her boyfriend answered, I asked for Lisa. Then, after a short pause, I said, "Oh shit, that's right, she's lying right next to me," laughed, and hung up.

"Why are you such an ass?" she said. (But she wasn't really mad.)

Well, she finally got rid of the turd and married a nice guy. She had a kid, and I was really happy for her because she always wanted a kid, and now she got what she wanted.

CHAPTER 25

BODY LANGUAGE

People are always saying to me, "Aren't you afraid of anything?" The truth is, I've been afraid all my life, but I react so quickly to any threat that I don't even see my own fear until it's over.

It was different when I was a kid, though. The first time I remember being actually scared was when I was about six. My parents found me hiding behind a chair in the front room, crying. They asked me what was wrong, and I said I fell and hurt myself. The truth was that the nuns in school had scared the shit out of me by always talking about the end of the world. I was always expecting the heavens to open up and rain fire. What a head trip to put on a kid!

When I was about seven, I came home and found my mom sleeping on the couch. I thought she was dead, and I just sat there crying because I didn't know what to do. She woke up and said, "What's wrong?" I just got up and went to my room.

Actually, my whole life I've spent my time afraid someone would find out I wasn't as tough as I seemed. Inside I was always a sensitive kid, a real nerd, but I was always pegged as a hardass because of the way I looked—big and tough. I never really fought unless I was forced to because I didn't like violence, and fortunately I could bullshit anybody in most situations.

A troublemaker, a nerd, or whatever you needed, I began to feel like a chameleon. But the truth is, if you keep acting a certain way, before you realize it, you get lost in your new persona, and that part you are hiding dies a little bit as well. So when I had to be brave—like getting on an airplane when I was scared of flying—the scared part just kept getting smaller. (Even though I kept thinking that maybe I would freak out and run up and down the aisle.)

There are times when you have to just stand up for what you believe, scared or not, and say, "Go for it." I finally realized it was better to die on your feet than live on your knees (unless you're a high-priced hooker). I guess they were right when they said a coward dies many deaths, but a brave man dies but once. It took me quite a while to learn this, but I did. If you have a problem, just meet it head-on—then it's over with and you don't spend needless time worrying about what's going to happen.

I remember one time in my life when I was really scared but covered it up. I was living in Vegas and had just rented an apartment in one of these three huge buildings at Stevenson and Twain. It was called the Blue Harbor Inn, and it looked pretty good when I saw it one Sunday afternoon, nice and quiet, so I paid three months' rent in advance, took a bus back to the casino, got my shit, and jumped in a cab. When I told the driver to take me to the Blue Harbor Inn, he asked me if I was crazy. "It's the worst place in Vegas for 911 calls," he said. "Not even the pizza men will deliver there after dark."

I told him it had been nice and quiet in the afternoon,

when I looked at it, and he laughed. "Of course," he said, "that was the *afternoon.* At night it's like a war zone." I was beginning to wonder, but I told him I'd lived in Compton in L.A. and Harlem with no problem, and on we went.

Well, I moved into my apartment in the middle of the third floor with a big patio door out to the balcony that ran along the side of the building. I did get the idea that I was the only white in the whole building. But I settled in, and when I got hungry later that night, I called about eight different places for takeout. They all said "No," even when I offered a $20 tip. I was thinking about what the cab driver had said, but I was still hungry.

Finally I remembered a 7-Eleven about a block away, and off I went. I picked up some SpaghettiOs, Twinkies, and milk, and headed home. I climbed up to the third floor and was headed toward my place when I noticed someone standing in the walkway and rap music blaring out from the apartment next door. I could feel my heartbeat pick up. I continued on. Then the figure, a big young black man who seemed more than a little toasted, said, "You got to pay a two-dollar toll."

"Yeah, sure," I said, and kept right on.

"I'm not kidding," he said.

I looked over to my left and noticed three of his friends sitting there laughing. "Get out of my way," I said.

He just stood there.

Now my heart was going a million miles a minute, but what could I do? If I gave in, I was going to get punked out and have to put up with this shit every time. If I didn't give in?—well, you only live once. If I was going out, I wasn't going alone.

I dropped my SpaghettiO's and grabbed him. Then I

swung around and tried to drop him over the rail down to the parking lot three stories below. But he was like a cat—his arms and legs were going every which way grabbing at me and wrapping around the railing. He was screaming, and his friends were yelling, "What the hell, you crazy son of a bitch!" I was just attending to business.

After several minutes, we agreed there was to be no toll, now or ever, and I let him go. All he kept saying as he hurried away was, "You crazy son of a bitch, what is wrong with you?"

I went inside and ate. My heart slowed down. And after that, whenever I came in and saw the guys, all they said was, "Hey, Big Man. How you doin', Big Man?" No more problems.

I'd been definitely scared that time, but I figured that even though I might get killed or tore up real bad, I had to take a stand or be punked and worried every time I came in and out. So I did. Most people figure that it's just easier to mess with someone else who won't put up a fight once they've learned that you'll fight back. It's the same in everyday life. No one knows if you're scared inside—I think the only times I wasn't was when I was numb from liquor or drugs.

I still get scared at not fitting in or people not liking me, but I have learned to cover it with bravado and just plow my way through.

CHAPTER 26

WHEN WORLDS COLLIDE

Jessica and Edie had been living in the duplex with me for about a year after their finances got tight, when I told them I'd take them to Vegas for a weekend. They weren't much interested in gambling, but I could show them the sights. I got a deal on the airfare, and I had enough play to get two suites at the Tropicana comped. I figured it was the least I could do after all the shit they'd put up with from me over the last thirty years.

Once we got there, it was great seeing everything through someone else's eyes. I took them to eat at the buffet at the Rio, the best in Vegas. Then I let them retire around 10 p.m. because the next day I was going to surprise them with a trip down to Laughlin, where the River Run was going on. It usually attracted about 30,000 to 40,000 bikers, like a mini-Sturgis but with casinos and a lot less people.

The ride down was great. It was Edie's and Jessica's first time to see the mountains and the desert, aside from on TV. They couldn't believe how beautiful everything was, and Edie said she could see why I loved it so much. Laughlin had bikes everywhere and lots of booths with everything for sale—shit, I never saw so much jewelry for sale in my life.

Actually, Edie had quite a time for not liking bikes and bikers, only once they ended up following the wrong guy for about twenty minutes before they found out it wasn't me. There were quite a few long-haired, tattooed bikers, go figure.

On the way back to Vegas, we saw the Hoover Dam, and I took them on the boat ride so they could really appreciate the beauty. When we got back to the Trop, I took them downtown for the light show on Fremont, and then to the Four Queens to see the Elvis impersonator. I even got to shoot a little craps and ended up winning about three grand. The next day, they wanted to just lay around the pool because I'd wore them out, and Sunday was pretty laid-back too, but I made sure they got to see the water show at the Bellagio and the pirate fight at Treasure Island, along with a stop at the Stardust, my favorite casino.

They had a great time until the airport incident on our way home. I always liked to get to the airport early, which was good because it was crazier than usual this time. As we sat there, Edie and Jess got up to go to the bathroom. I was saving their places for them, but this guy sat down right in their seats. "I'm saving the seats for someone who just went to the bathroom," I said.

"Well, they're not here now—I'll move when they get back," he said.

After several minutes, Edie and Jess came back, but they sat in the two open seats across the aisle from me. I told the guy that they're back. "Would you switch seats now?" I said, trying to be polite.

But he tells me, "Hey, I'm not moving, so just deal with it."

I looked at Jess and Edie and could see the look of dread. They thought I was going to go off, but, shit, there were 100

witnesses around, so I just bit my bottom lip and sat there stewing, thinking, You Bernard Goetz–looking dick. Well, after about fifteen minutes, he got up and I saw him walk into the restroom. Then I realized nature was calling, so off I went, too. I walked in, and it was totally empty except for Mr. Smartass at the urinal.

Well, I strolled up to him and said, "Hey." As he turned around, I said, "This is how I deal with it," and hit him so hard his head bounced off the tile wall, and he hit the floor pissing all over himself. I grabbed him and dragged him into a stall, and as he started to come to, I bitch-slapped him and proceeded to put his head in the toilet. After all, he was being a shithead.

Well, I left him in the stall and washed my hands and went back to my seat feeling a lot better after answering a call of nature. We sat there for forty-five more minutes, and I never saw him come out—we boarded our flight never seeing him again. When we got back home and settled in, Jess and Edie were saying what a great trip it was and they were so impressed how I handled the situation at the airport. (If only they knew.)

CHAPTER 27

SEEKING

Religion is one thing that I think is so misunderstood and misinterpreted. Even as a small child, I really had issues with the way the Catholic Church and most organized religions had no tolerance for anyone who was not of that belief. The God I learned about was kind and loving, but it seemed religion always threatened you with one bad thing after another if you weren't perfect. I figured that God, being all-seeing and -knowing, knew right away what people were like inside, and he just wants us to do the best we can.

I really get a kick out of these religions who believe theirs is the only path to God. Why can't they understand we are all trying to achieve the same goals whether we're talking to Jesus, Allah, or Buddha, because they're all essentially the same person? Things have been so twisted over the years, and the people in power realized the best way to control everyone was through religion that their leaders could interpret—whether through the Bible, Koran, or whatever—to fit their needs.

We have all been taught to judge not lest you be judged, but nowadays the Bible, Koran, and Torah have been turned into weapons by people who have their own agendas, whether it be keeping infidels off holy land or keeping gays from marrying. We even have people who are preaching that our soldiers are being killed because the USA is tolerant of gays. When are we going to wake up and see we were all put here to learn to get along and live in peace? What if all these different religions were started by a Supreme Being as just another test, and he can't believe how we are all killing and persecuting each other in his name? I'm sure he's just sitting there thinking, What the f***? How can you get this so wrong?

I remember when I had my real epiphany. I had always felt like I was so bad and there was no way I was going to be saved—until one Sunday my daughter Jessica asked me for a ride to church. I dropped her off and said I'd wait, but she said, "Why not come in?" After several minutes of being nagged, I thought, Yeah, why not? Well, as usual, walking in made me feel that I didn't belong here. I wasn't comfortable. But I sat down, and when they got to the Gospel, I was sort of half listening when the priest started talking about the Prodigal Son. It hit me—I thought, Holy shit, if that doesn't sound familiar. Then I realized what I had been longing for all these years, the thing I couldn't find with drugs, booze, money, sex, something that was so simple all I had to do was open up my heart to God and realize I was okay. I was just human.

From that moment on, I became calmer and really tried to be more accepting of the things around me. I realized I could actually like myself, which I never did before—and I always figured if I didn't like me, how could anyone else? The more I prayed for inner peace, the more my eyes were opened. I still had trouble with a lot of the politics of the church, but I held on to the fundamentals. I started to learn more and more about other religions, and I worked on being more open to other philosophies.

Then I got into Buddhism. It seemed so perfect—no reward for being good because being good was its own reward. It was the understanding that no one person's joy or sorrow is more important than anyone else's. You are trying to become a more enlightened person, and by being more compassionate to others you enrich your own life. You stop worrying about being first, the toughest, the richest—you realize you are no better than anyone else and no one else is better than you. You start to realize every action you take affects other people. It's like throwing a rock into a pond—the way the ripples touch, so do all our lives. So what if your neighbor is gay and has a partner and wants to share his or her life? What effect does that really have on you except when you get all worked up and judgmental and lose sleep and are all enraged? Wasn't that person made by the same person who made you? Aren't we all taught to love one another and not judge each other? Wouldn't life be so much easier if we concentrated on being the best person we could be and not be so worried about everyone else? After all, we will all be standing alone to be judged. There's not going to be any witnesses or prosecuting attorneys. It's just him knowing what was in our heart and how we acted on it, whether in love or hatred of something we didn't understand or like.

I remember one of the most spiritual experiences I had. About a year after I started getting into Buddhism, I was working at the Roseville V.F.W., and I was reading the morning paper when I came across the article about His Holiness, the Dalai Lama. I said, "Shit, he would really be a great person to meet."

Karla Miller, who was the manager, said, "He really is a great man, and funny, too."

I shot back, "Yeah, like you know him."

And she said, "Well, it just so happens I do." She told me how her parents were professors at the University of Wisconsin in Madison, and they lived in India for several years when she was young. She had met the Dalai Lama on several occasions, and her parents were instrumental in building Deer Park, the temple in Madison.

I freaked out and said, "If he ever comes anywhere near here, hook me up if you can." Then about four months later, I was in Las Vegas for a month when she called me and said I had to be back because His Holiness was coming to town and she had tickets. I came right back, and we went to his first lecture at the university. We had great seats—I mean, we were about 100 feet from where he was going to sit.

As it happened, we were there so early that I decided to go outside to the concession stand to get a pop. When I got there, there were two people working like crazy, and there were five lines of at least ten people deep. I couldn't believe what was going on because everyone was bitching and complaining about how long this was taking. They weren't concerned at all for the two people busting their asses to wait on them. I thought, Hey, work on your mantra. Think about all the nice things that happened to you today. Shit, they were acting like they were waiting to see WWF Wrestling, not the man who teaches the value of compassion toward your fellow human beings. Here I was probably the most violence-prone person there, and I was working on my mantra and praying for them to mellow out.

His lecture was great. He is so calm and modest. He's not trying to convert everyone to Buddhism—he said you have to go with what is the most comfortable for you and just try to live your life with compassion and understanding for everyone. Do not lose all the calm and serenity harboring hatred for others.

Then afterward Karla took me up to him and we bowed to each other. I met some of the other Buddhist teachers, too. I've never experienced anything like it in my life.

CHAPTER 28

THE ACCIDENT

It was the afternoon of April 21, 2001, when the world as I knew it came crashing down. I was at work at the Roseville V.F.W. getting ready for a wedding I was catering. The food was ready to go into the oven when I decided to pick up some extra rolls. (I was always worried about running out of food.)

On the way back, only three blocks from work, I saw a van coming in the opposite direction start to cross the center line and drift into my lane. It's funny how fast your mind processes information—I thought about speeding up to pass him, about swerving into his lane to get past him that way, about jumping the curb into a yard, and about hitting him head-on. All of that took about three seconds, and I was halfway up the curb when he hit me right behind the driver's door. The crash pushed me sideways into a large tree. I remember the initial hit, but then I lost consciousness.

When I came to, I remember people asking me if I was all right. My head was aching on the left side where it had broken the side window, and I had a super large bump in back of my head where I'd hit the door trim after I spun in the seat belt and hit the tree. I was confused and shaken, but all I could think about was the wedding. I figured that if there was no blood and nothing was sticking out, I must be okay.

Someone from the V.F.W. happened to be driving by about then. He went and told my brother Bill, who had been helping me, what had happened, and he showed up before the ambulance asking how I was. I just kept saying, "The wedding!" and he told me not to worry—he and his wife, Betty, would handle everything.

When the ambulance came, the medics checked me out. Against their advice, I went back with Bill to the V.F.W. Everything went great—all I did was lay in the back room with a killer headache. Then, after everything was done, Bill insisted on taking me to the ER, where I waited a couple of hours (it was a Saturday night) before a doctor finally came. He looked at my eyes, felt my head, and said that since it had happened over twelve hours before, if it was anything serious, I would be dead by now anyway. Then he left the room. I thought he was joking, but in twenty minutes a nurse came in with my discharge papers. I guess it was the old "treat and street," especially since I didn't have any insurance.

Later, after numerous trips to my own doctor, a chiropractor, an MRI and a CAT scan, and a workup by a neurologist (my car insurance paid for all this), I found out I had three herniated disks in my neck, a headache that wouldn't go away, and, as they put it, slight brain damage. I'd worked my way through car and motorcycle accidents, overcome my fear of heights, kicked my drug and drinking habits, so I couldn't believe that I wouldn't be able to work through this. But after eight months (during which my restaurant business at the V.F.W. went down the tube), I was still having trouble

with my speech, and I had become really withdrawn. I'd use the wrong word and forget what I was talking about. I'd always been the go-to guy who could solve your problems, and now I couldn't even organize my desk. The headaches hadn't gotten any better, and I didn't like taking anything for them because of my drug history. I'd had a great memory before the accident, but now I forgot people's names, phone numbers, everything. It was devastating.

Fortunately, I had a good doctor, and she saw that I was going deeper and deeper into depression. She tried me on different meds and got me to where I could see a therapist. I had to learn to accept who I was now and change my values. I learned that if I really concentrated, my speech got a lot better, and I learned to use an organizer and write things down so I wouldn't forget. I had a hard time being around crowds, but I worked on the panic attacks and they got better.

Almost a year after the accident, I started driving again. I made myself drive to Vegas alone, something I'd done many times before the accident. This was real work, though. I don't know how many times I started to turn around, but I made it and met Butch there. I also found out my card-playing ability was gone, and the machines with all their lights and noise drove me crazy. So I saw a lot of the sights instead. I even stopped in Winslow, Arizona, to stand on a corner just like in the song.

When I got back, I tried to go back to the V.F.W., but it didn't work out. I'd run kitchens, done all the ordering, run the staff on autopilot, but now I had to write down little things like when dishes had to come out of the oven. Once at the V.F.W. I'd done a wedding for 140 people downstairs and a golf banquet for 75 people upstairs with just one waitress helping me. But those days were gone.

After the accident, Butch had always kept in touch and tried to get me out and about. He never gave up. We were even making plans to go to the World Series of Poker in Vegas to play in the satellites, but little did I know Butch would pass away two weeks before the series. Then Vegas was the last place I wanted to be.

Finally, when things settled down after Butch's death, I heard that Sandy was going to sell the shop, Butch's Custom, and I volunteered to go up there and keep an eye on things. I figured it would be good for the customers to see an old familiar face. Doing this really helped me—I felt I was doing something to show Butch how much I appreciated all the things he'd done. I met Mike Anderson, the gentleman who was buying Butch's, and we hit it off right away. He told me to call him Cripple Mike because he had lost a leg in a motorcycle accident several years earlier, and he now rode an FX that was all tricked out. A lot of people give it up after a little accident, but he was a real rider.

After several weeks I started to feel better around people and almost like the old Deadeye. I couldn't remember the jokes like I used to or the people's names, but everything else seemed all right. A lot of the brothers from the club were stopping up to visit me, and Mother Mick also came to help. Butch had hired a mechanic named Larry who was good but needed direction—every so often he needed to get tuned up just like the bikes.

While I was there, I thought about building a bike of my own. I'd sold the one I bought before the accident when Butch, his three brothers, and me went to Vegas for the

Super Bowl, and I picked up about $5,000 from playing cards for a down payment. I was supposed to go down in May to ride it back, but after the accident, I was in no shape to do that. I had it shipped back to Butch's in Saint Paul, and he sold it for me.

Now I wanted to build an Evo chopper, and I started to line up parts. But my budget was really tight, and when Mike Anderson (I just can't call him "Cripple") heard about my predicament, he asked me if I wanted to borrow $6,000. "You've only known me about a month," I said, but he'd heard stories about me, and he knew my word was good enough. (But he did make me sign a contract.) I couldn't believe how fast the bike came together—I got some real smoking deals from the distributors when they heard I was building a bike in tribute to Butch. I picked up an engine, tranny, and electric start set-up from Butch's brother, Robert.

The bike was completed two days before the Aldrich Arena show, which was the last show Butch had had a bike in just before his death. We got it entered and all detailed by Todd at the Downtowner Car Wash. It looked great—bright red, with BUTCH and NEVER FORGOTTEN on the gas tank. I set up a display with Butch's picture from last year's show—he was holding the trophy and money he'd won—along with a bottle of Southern Comfort with a Bourbon Bar shot glass. I know he got a kick out of it, especially when we won first place in our class.

I've come a long way since the accident. I'm not the same as I was, but now I'm getting to know and like the new me.

CHAPTER 29

BUT A FEW

It's funny—you really don't realize the effect you have on people sometimes, or the effect they have on you. When I was working at Butch's, there was this young kid, about nineteen, named Ryan. He never had a bike but was trying to build one, but he'd gotten ripped off at a swap meet by a real piece of shit who sold him a Honda frame saying it was a Harley. He'd come in and ask all these questions. There was just something different about him. Butch and the guys would give me shit about all the time I spent trying to help him out and just bullshitting about bikes and the club. Ryan just had that spark. We were all young once.

Well, he ended up getting a Sportster Hardtail together, and he'd stop by the shop with it. As he grew, everyone else saw that spark and paid him more attention. Maybe we all saw that part of us in him. After about a year, people were giving him shit about prospecting, and he came to me and said he didn't think he was ready. I told him he was the only one who really knew when it's right, and to go by his feelings. About four months later, he came into the club and made his patch. He's one of the best brothers I've had.

All the stories don't work out like that, though. When I

had my shop on Concord, Billy the Kid used to drop in. (That's what we called him because he was only about twelve.) We used to have him clean up the parking lot and take out the trash. Then, when he was fifteen, he fell in love with a piece-of-shit Sportster we had in the back room. It hadn't run in years, but the way the kid treated it, you'd think it was a show bike. I gave him a deal and let him work on it when I was around, and Butch did some freebie engine work. Shit, before long it was running and looking pretty good.

Well, Billy the Kid had the bike about half paid for, including all the new things he'd added, when he got busted for selling drugs. I couldn't believe it—he was only fifteen. He had to do juvenile time, and when I visited him, I told him not to worry, the bike was waiting for him. After about one and a half years, he got out, and he hit the ground running with the drugs. I was dealing then, too, but I tried to talk him into a different vocation—he was just too young to ruin his life. He said, yeah, he'd seen the error of his ways, but he still continued to deal.

After about two years, he sold the Sporty and got a real sharp FLH. He started to hang around the club, and then he started prospecting with us. I was still on him about the dealing, but the money was just too good for him. He couldn't understand why I wouldn't deal with him or to him, but I'd look at him and see that kid who used to clean up the parking lot.

Not long after he made patch, he got busted again. He went to Saint Cloud for several years, still owing me money for the bike work and legal fees. I took his title and got the bike out of the impound lot—why let the cops have it? They charged me about $900 in storage fees. Butch and I visited him and kept in touch with his parents.

When he finally got out, I'd hoped he had learned how to run his life. He came back to the club, prospected again, and made patch. But he was on a mission to make up for lost time and money—he got so far out there he wasn't listening to anyone, so we had to part ways. Me and Butch were really disappointed the way he turned out—even with all the help we tried to give him, he was lost. He went to another club, but they saw how out of control he was, and then he was on his own. Sure as shit, he took another bust—this time it was nineteen years. What a waste. But I'll give him credit—he took the time and never snitched. That says a lot in my book.

Beaver was another person who made my attitude change—but in the opposite direction. He's a six-foot-three long-haired party animal, and he was in the Los Valientes before me. When I started prospecting, he really didn't like me, but he took a shine to me after a while. His sense of humor is a real trip—once a guy was bitching about a motorcycle accident he'd had ten years earlier when he'd lost his leg. After about two hours, Beav broke in and said, "That's a real bitch, but it could have been worse. It could have been me."

I've always been fortunate to have Beav as my vice president when I've been president of the Los Valientes, and he's done a good job, party animal or not. Because we were a team, I made up the slogan, "Dick (my real name) and Beaver, one f***ing thing after another." I still don't know his real first name, but who cares? It works just the way it is.

Then there's Tommy, or Tommy Gun, or the Rebel, Butch's youngest brother. Tommy is the most intense person

I know. The first time I met him, I was hanging around a bar with the Valientes. There were about twenty-five regulars in there, and some shit started. Tommy was outside, and he wanted Tooter and Mongo to throw him through the window into the bar. He said, "Man, that will really freak them out," and the look on his face and his smile and the way his eyes were on fire, I knew he wasn't kidding. Well, they didn't, but eight Valientes and one hangaround freaked those suckers out just by using the door. Tommy's the kind of person who believes in you 100 percent and is there forever, but God help you if you're on his bad side. A badger would look like a bunny compared to the Rebel.

One of my oldest biker friends is Mother Mick. (How he got the "Mother" part of his name has several stories connected with it, but I'm passing.) We met back in '63 when I was hanging around downtown, and then we ended up in the same motorcycle club.

Mick is the kind of guy who knows everyone. No matter where we go, he's always running into some relative or friend. He's also the neatest person I know—everything is always in place, clean and organized. We always give him shit about how clean he keeps everything. If anyone has the gift of gab, he does—his ancestors must have had something to do with planting the Blarney Stone. Mick is only one year older than me, fifty-seven, but he's always got some young hottie hanging around. We could never figure it out, when finally I realized his secret—he talks them into submission and just wears them down.

One of the funniest stories about Mick is the time we were on a run to Duluth to the Blues Festival. Another brothers, Lefty, was with this young girl named Crystal, who was riding on the back of his Hardtail. He was running shotgun pipes, and the right passenger foot peg was right under the pipe. Crystal had on sandals, and her foot got really hot on the way up—she did a lot of bitching about it.

Well, when we got to the campground, one of our other brothers, Ramone, hooks up with her, and I started giving Lefty shit about how he pumped up the tires but Ramone's riding the bike. He said, "Forget her, too much drama." As it happened, in the morning Ramone took off with another chick he'd met, and then Crystal was in need of a ride. Well, Lefty's a real gentleman, so he said he'd give her a ride home, but she starts bitching about how hot the pipe was on her foot. So Mother Mick comes up with this idea to wrap her foot in tinfoil to deflect the heat. Sounded good to everyone, so the foot is wrapped.

On the way home, though, her big toe got baked like a potato. I mean, all you needed was butter and sour cream—I couldn't believe it. She ended up in the hospital, and it took about three months for her toe to heal. To this day, Mother Mick gets a lot of shit about his baking abilities.

Another brother is Gaylord. I've known him almost as long as Mother Mick. We also met in downtown Saint Paul on the Loop back in the '60s, through mutual friends. We were at a party, and he was going out with a girl I knew. I had always heard about this crazy Indian, and shit, the stories weren't even close. He could drink and smoke anyone I'd known under the table, and he was a real ladies' man besides—he was with a new girl every time I saw him.

One day, after not seeing each other for about ten years, I ran into him, Mongo, Butch, Eddy Dog, Michael, and Jimmy Jam at a gas station on White Bear and Seventh. They told me about this club they were starting, the Los Valientes, and I couldn't believe all the guys I'd hung around with at

different times in my life were all together in this. I wasn't surprised to see Gaylord was still the ladies' man—shit, he's the only person I know who would get one girlfriend to babysit for another girlfriend's kids so he could go out with the second one.

Gaylord was quite a rider, too. He rode this Hardtail chopper, and the funniest story I'd heard about his riding was the time him and about twenty of the guys went to Sturgis, and he was in town drinking, smoking, and cruising. Well, he got separated from everyone, and he was beating feet back to the campground through all these winding roads when he lost control and crashed. He slid off and the bike kept going. He just laid there for about ten minutes taking inventory—everything was okay, but it was dark, and he couldn't find his bike.

Finally someone came by and gave him a ride back to camp to get some help. As the sun started to break, the guys all took off to rescue his bike. When they got to the spot, they saw there was about a ten-foot cliff with skid marks and scrapes into the turn, but no bike. Gaylord started yelling and swearing, "Piece of shit bike thieves!" when someone looked across to this group of trees about eight feet from the cliff, and wedged in them was Gaylord's chopper like a giant Christmas ornament. It took two tow trucks and $500 to get the bike down, but that's small change for such a great crash story.

And then there's Tooter. Back in '82, Butch got this call from Gaylord that some crazy monster up at the Bourbon Bar where we hung out was just standing there drinking and beating the bar with his chain drive belt until he was almost through the top. It was like a chain saw. Butch and some of the other guys showed up, and they had a quick meeting and figured either they had to prospect this guy or shoot him, and the rest is club history. Later, two prospects we had who were both big boys, Maniac and Dan, thought they were going to teach Tooter a lesson, just a little innocent wrestling to show him who's the boss. Well, later I got a call to go to Ramsey Hospital to pick them up because they had just gotten out of the ER.

Actually, I'd known Tooter back from junior high when his name was Jeff Mickelson. I'd lost track of him, and the new Tooter was about six-foot-four, 300 pounds, and one of the meanest people I've ever known if he was provoked. I mean, I'd rather poke a bear in the nose with a stick than piss off Tooter. It's funny—the madder he got, the quieter he talked. I think it was so whoever he was talking to would get closer to hear—and then, wham, he had them. But we never had a cross word between us. He was one that I'd trust with my kids.

One of the saddest things I had to deal with was Tooter's death from liver cancer. As I sat there at the service, I thought if anyone ever deserved a Viking funeral, it was my brother Tooter, the warrior.

CHAPTER 30

VAYA CON DIOS

On March 26, 2003, I got the call from Tommy, Butch's younger brother. He told me Butch had had a stroke and to get up to the hospital on Beam Avenue right away.

I was across town, so I came as fast as I could. I just kept telling myself, "Hey, that's Butch, everything's going to be okay. My grandfather had four strokes and he got through them—and this is Butch, no problem." But the drive seemed like it took four times longer than it should have.

As I got to the hospital and was going in, I ran into Rochelle, Butch's youngest daughter. She looked so upset. "It really looks bad," she said.

I said, "It's Butch, he's going to be okay," and I really believed it.

But as I came off the elevator, I had a feeling of dread. Tommy was there, along with Robert (who was number four in that family of five kids). "It's bad, it really is," they both said, and they took me into the room.

When I saw Butch lying in that bed, he looked so vulnerable. I'd never seen Butch like that, not once in our lives together. He was in a coma. I felt scared, and I remembered when my father had his heart attack. That was the last time

I'd felt that fear. Dad was only forty-two and had always been skinny and athletic. In fact, the docs thought he was doing all right, too, and they took him out of the ICU. But that night he died, and my brother Joe called to tell me. For years, the sound of a phone ringing at night gave me cold sweats, and I couldn't talk about my father's death with anyone for nearly five years. Now here I was looking at Butch and praying, "Not him."

Butch was my best friend. Just days before, we were talking about going to Vegas to play in the satellites for the World Series of Poker. I was always kidding him about my nightmare that he and I were at the final table, and I knew I didn't stand a chance against him. I was so psyched out when it came to playing cards with him that I always lost. And now all I wanted was for him to beat my straight flush with a royal like only he could do.

This was such a private and personal thing that I felt like I was intruding. Sandy, Butch's wife, was crying, and I wanted to go up and hug her and say, "It's going to be okay," but who was I? I was just numb. Robert, Tommy, and me were standing alongside Butch's bed, and I reached out and took his hand. I thought how massive his arms were, even laying there, and I studied his tattoos even though I'd seen them for years. Robert said, "Butch, Deadeye's here, and he's holding your hand," and all of a sudden Butch gave my hand a squeeze. It caught me off guard, and I jumped. Then I bent down and whispered in his ear, "I'm here, you're going to be okay. I know Mongo, Tooter, Doc, and Stan aren't ready for you yet." (They were brothers in the club who'd already passed.) Then he squeezed my hand again, and I swear he could hear us and was letting us know.

I looked around the room and thought how plain it was,

definitely not what Butch was used to, no fruit basket or wide screen TV, not a high roller suite. It just wasn't right. Then I looked back at Sandy and Bonnie (one of Sandy's three daughters who Butch had raised) and felt so helpless, wishing I could say something (I was the one who always had something smart to say) but not having a clue. I stood there for about twenty minutes longer holding his hand and talking—and getting a squeeze at times that seemed to fit what I was saying.

I wanted to say, "Make your peace with God," just in case, but I didn't want to seem like an idiot. I wanted to say how much I cared for him and loved him like the true brother he was to me, and thank him for everything. But no, I couldn't, because after all you have to put up this image of always acting hard. But here was the best friend I ever had, and I still just didn't want to say how I really felt. But I know he knew how I felt.

I think my mind just shut down because I really don't remember much until I got back to the hospital the next day. The family said Butch had had a bad night and there was no brain activity. I just stood there numb, saying how sorry I was to Sandy, Tommy, and Robert, but what good was that? I was just like a lump standing, sitting, not knowing.

We waited for a doctor to come and talk to the family. When he came, we went out in the hall, and he told everyone that Butch's brain wasn't functioning and he wasn't going to come back. I just kept hearing, "Butch is gone." Shit, that ain't right! We had always planned on getting old together, him and Sandy moving to Vegas and me coming down so we could go into the catering business together. And the gambling and all the bullshit we had to do—we were so good at it we even got to believe some of our own stories.

Then I looked around the room and thought how sorry I feel can't be anything compared to Sandy, the kids, Robert, Tommy, and Gene, the third brother. They were blood family, and I was just a friend. Then I heard the doctor say something about taking Butch off life support. What a choice to make! It's so hard to be strong and make the decision Butch would want, and not just want him here with that false hope he would get better.

Then the decision was made, and we all went back in the room to say our last good-byes and wait for the doctor to come back in and proceed. I stood there for a while and felt like I was going crazy. I wanted to yell, but I figured I had to leave. I didn't want to lose it and put any more stress on the family, so I told Robert and Tommy I couldn't stay, hugged Sandy, and left, waiting for the call that Butch was really gone.

I just sat in my truck for what seemed like hours, then drove around just remembering all the shit we did and how just a few weeks before I'd told Butch how much I missed the road trips to Vegas. I was cursing the last two years since my car accident when I rarely saw Butch because I was all screwed up with the head injury and the depression I was in. But Butch still kept in touch, checking on me, and I could still hear him say, "Heeeyyy, Deadeye," like he used to say every time I called the shop. I just kept playing it over and over again in my head.

When the call came that he was gone, Robert said that though the doctor thought it would be ten or fifteen minutes, it had been over a half hour. If anyone could fight to the finish, it was Butch.

The next days were a fog. All the "I can't believe he's gone's" and the "I'm so sorry's," they just melted into one. At

the wake there were a lot of people and some great flowers. I could see Butch looking down going, "Mm, not too bad." All the club was there, including a lot of retired members, and many people who had been kicked out or never made it, and a lot of other motorcycle clubs. Everyone showed up to pay their respect to Butch, the husband, father, brother, mechanic extraordinaire, and one badass motherf***er.

Then came the funeral. I was going to ride a bike Butch had built that was at the shop because I had sold mine after the car accident. (I needed something to ride in the procession up to the cemetery after the funeral.) I had to ride no matter what. Well, I was two blocks from the shop when the clutch cable broke. I nursed it back to the shop, then took a custom bike, and I rode about three blocks when it got a flat tire. Back to the shop I went. It was getting late, and I had to be at the clubhouse to meet everyone and go to the church. Robert showed up, though, and said I could ride a prospect's bike, so off I went.

I got to the church. It was kind of cloudy, and everyone was saying they hoped the weather would cooperate, but I knew Butch, and if he could, he would get it to rain on us. I was so touched when Sandy asked me to sit with the family—that was one of the most moving things anyone ever said to me. I felt so good to be thought of in that way, but I said I had to be a pallbearer, and I sat across the aisle with the rest of the brothers.

The service was beautiful, even though my cell went off and everyone was looking around saying, "What the hell?" I grabbed it and said Butch was calling, telling me that it was going to rain and not to ride his bike in it. I finally got to see Mary, the writer I had heard so much about—the lady with the cookies—because she gave the eulogy. Then the pallbearers walked up the aisle behind Butch for the last time.

After that, we had the procession following the hearse. There must have been 200 motorcycles. When we got to the graveyard, we saw that Butch had a nice corner plot, but up the hill behind it was all the Alphabet Squad—FBI, DEA, BOA—filming just to see who showed up. Biker funerals are real interesting for them because a lot of people come out of the woodwork. Everyone was bitching, "What the hell, he's dead, why can't they let him rest in peace?" I just chuckled to myself because I knew that if they weren't there, Butch would have been disappointed and pissed, because that would show no respect.

When all the words were said and people had started to go, we said our final good-bye to our brother. Sandy, Rochelle, and all the rest stood around the grave. We had a bottle of Los Valientes tequila and several bottles of Southern Comfort. We spilled a little in the grave for Butch, and then we all took turns, first taking a drink and then shoveling dirt in on the coffin. No backhoe—we did it ourselves. And then as everyone left on their bikes, they burned out on the blacktop in front of Butch's grave. I could hear him saying, "You guys are voiding your warranty on engine work. I've got tires on sale, though."

Later we all met up at the Roseville V.F.W. where I handled the food. I did Mexican (Butch liked it) and made 1,000 deep-fried tacos, but we still ran out. I said I would have done that many tacos only for Butch, and Robert said, "Wouldn't you do that for me?" I paused, acting like I was thinking, and replied, "Sure, because there wouldn't be as many people."

The party afterward was full of Butch stories, pictures,

and lots of love for one of a kind. Then, several days after the funeral, I found myself at Treasure Island, a local casino Butch and I used to go to, and headed for the dollar video poker machines that we used to play. About $40 into the machine, I'm dealt a king, queen, and jack of hearts, which I hold, and up pops a ten and ace of hearts for a royal flush. My first reaction is to turn and tell Butch, "Hey, I got your machine." Then I realize, and look at that royal, and say, "Thanks."

Afterword

Well, that's it—the good, the bad, and the ugly. Writing this book was a great cleansing. I'd like to thank Mary Gardner, without whose help and totally non-judgmental attitude this book would still be rambling around in my head. Who would have thought I'd become best friends with a seventy-year-old college English teacher and author? My brother Butch made my life a lot more interesting even after his passing when he still managed to introduce the two of us.

I'd also like to thank my friend and lawyer (a true oxymoron) Roger (The Shark) Alderson, for legal advice on statutes of limitation. He told me it's seven and a half years for everything except kidnapping and murder, which have no limits for prosecution. So I left out those two chapters.

I've taken many paths and grown a lot as a person, as I've come to realize. I've always wondered why, after two shootings, one stabbing, a snake bite, a scorpion bite, numerous car and motorcycle accidents, and even two marriages, I'm still around. Probably it's to show only the good do die young.

I hope this book opened up at least a small part of my world to you. Thanks.

—The person your parents warned you about,
Deadeye